The Sewists

The Sewists

*DIY Projects from
20 Top Designer-Makers*

Josephine Perry

LAURENCE KING PUBLISHING

LAURENCE KING

Published in 2014 by
Laurence King Publishing Ltd

361–373 City Road
London EC1V 1LR
United Kingdom
Tel: +44 20 7841 6900
Fax: +44 20 7841 6910
e-mail: enquiries@laurenceking.com
www.laurenceking.com

A catalogue record for this book is
available from the British Library.

ISBN: 978-1-78067-182-6

Design by Jane Chipchase-Bates
Step-by-step illustrations by Lily Tennant
Photography of book projects by Sam Walton
Photography on page 33 by Emma Collins
Photography on page 42 by Dianne Tanner and Sarah Carr

Printed in China

Contents

Josephine Perry

My name is Josephine Perry and I sew things. Growing up, I destroyed perfectly good garments with a pair of dressmaking scissors, blundering my way through freestyle stitches to no useful end. Watching my mum lay out beautiful prints on the living-room floor and laboriously hand stitch lining to curtain fabric, I thought I'd never be cut out for sewing. Then I grew up, and in the idle hours of my twenties I started making again. This time, intrigued by the process, I wanted to acquire the skills to sew properly. I had the sense that something was happening, that others were sewing too, and then I discovered that craft had become a 'thing' once more. Since I am a maker and admire the work of those who create daily, *The Sewists* was born out of my crafting curiosity and desire to connect with other creative people. The tactile quality of good design and the importance of a considered choice of materials and colour in accomplished sewing is undeniable. From the moment we see great work on the page or screen we want to be able to touch it. In these pages I meet exciting and inspirational sewists, experience their workspaces, understand their creative adventures and share with you their sewing projects, based on the particular techniques that feature in their work.

Each designer-maker shared her skill with great generosity, dissecting her creations step by step to enable me to re-create her work. Each project is designed to address particular sewing skills, requiring some preparation, time and dexterity for a gratifying result.

In this collection of the work of designer-makers I admire, with creations I covet, I hope those who sew will discover new ideas, try out techniques and delve further into the world of sewing.

With affection for mid-century style and Liberty prints,
my ideas originate at home in the workroom.

Heritage Pincushion

JOSEPHINE PERRY

The tomato pincushion has been a sewing-box staple for generations, evocative of the hands-on lifestyle of the past. Many myths surround the seemingly odd choice of a tomato for pin storage. I choose to believe that in days gone by, the tomato symbolized the harvest, a reminder of the good things that follow skilled work – a little bit like sewing itself.

1.

Prepare Materials
Using the compasses, draw and cut out a circle measuring 16cm *(6¼in)* in diameter from the main fabric. Do the same with the iron-on interfacing; this time the circle should measure 14cm *(5½in)* in diameter. Iron the interfacing on to the wrong side of the fabric (this will help to strengthen it against the pins).

MATERIALS

Pair of compasses and pencil.

Cotton fabric measuring at least 17 x 17cm *(6¾ x 6¾in)*, plus an extra small piece.

Iron-on interfacing measuring at least 15 x 15cm *(5⅞ x 5⅞in)*.

Needle and thread.

Polyester stuffing.

Self-cover button.

Scrap paper.

Small piece of plain felt.

Emery sand or rice (optional).

General Knowledge
The traditional tomato pincushion was packed with wool or hair, the oil of which would keep the pins from rusting. A small fabric strawberry containing emery sand was often attached to keep pins sharp. Although this is not necessary in the age of stainless steel, the sand adds a satisfying weight.

To add weight to the pincushion, create a small pouch by sewing two rectangles of cotton fabric together on three sides, and carefully fill with the sand or rice. Use fabric glue to secure the opening, then when dry add a few stitches to strengthen. When filling the pincushion, put the pouch of sand in the centre and surround it with stuffing.

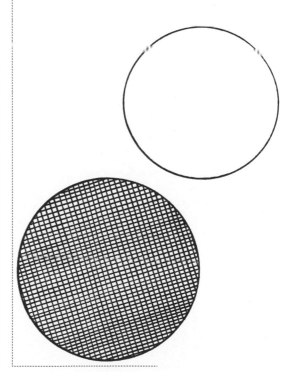

2.

Stitch and Gather
Thread a needle with a
single thread, without tying
a knot in the end. Sew a
line of stitches around the
edge of the outer fabric,
leaving a long tail. Make
sure the stitches are of even
length: about 1cm *(⅜in)*,
with a gap of about half
that between them.

   When you have sewn
all the way around, pull
on both ends of the thread
gently to gather the fabric,
leaving a gap at the top.

3.

Stuff and Secure
Layer some stuffing at
the bottom of the tomato,
working with small pieces
to ensure a good finish.
It should be densely filled.
Pull the thread tails again
and tie tightly several
times to secure. You can
even stitch over them for
added security.

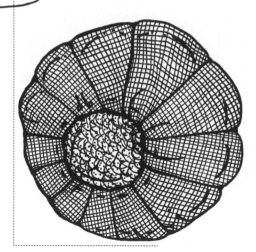

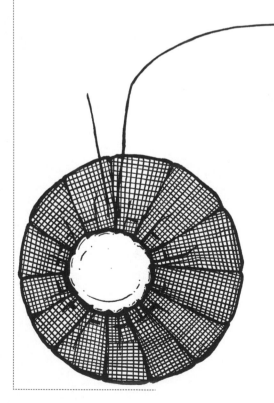

4.

Button and Leaf
Using a small piece of
the main fabric, create a
covered button following
the instructions supplied
on the reverse of the
packet. Make a template
for the leaf by drawing
a simple shape on scrap
paper, then pin it to the
felt and cut out.

5.

**Assemble Base,
Leaf and Button**
Attach the covered
button to the centre of
the leaf. Place the leaf on
top of the gathered base,
and either pin and stitch
it in place or glue it using
fabric adhesive.

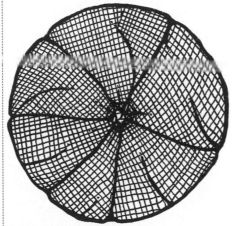

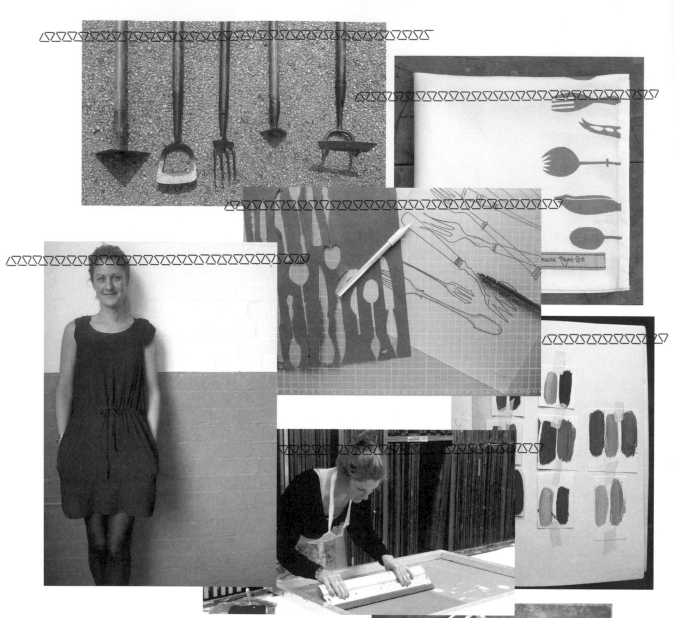

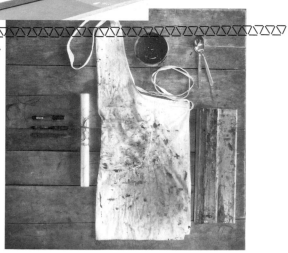

Jessica Hayes-Gill

Hand-Printed Textile Designer

Jessica Hayes-Gill's home-centric and design-led work is a celebration of the everyday paraphernalia of the kitchen. Working from her studio in Nottingham, she produces homewares from original hand-drawn designs, carefully researched and made into printed textiles. Each object is functional and evocative of time spent around the dining table sharing a meal.

Jessica studied graphic arts and design, specializing in print, before going on to set up her own business. Taking advantage of further training and internship opportunities enabled her to understand the way different designers operate their businesses. Jessica appreciates the importance of continued learning and experience, and applies the same approach to her research.

Inspired by the craftsmanship that went into the invention of knives, forks and spoons, Jessica visited the factory of David Mellor, Royal Designer for Industry. There, she encountered an abundance of cutlery (flatware) and kitchen equipment in shapes that she was keen to replicate in print.

Drawn to the heritage of British manufacturing, Jessica keeps her production local, using her studio facilities and local machinists to create her kitchen accessories. She cites the textile designs of Lucienne Day as a key influence on her work; she admires the abstract nature of Day's designs and the practical spirit of her legacy. Jessica's works start life as a series of sketches, which are developed into hand-cut stencils. She translates this work to cloth by screen printing. She delights in the processes and results of textile and interior design, and uses the prolific output of Conran and Marimekko as a benchmark.

Tools and cutlery, colour and paint: Jessica Hayes-Gill creates screen-printed textiles in her Nottingham studio.

Four Seasons Block-Printed Napkins

JESSICA
HAYES-GILL

This project is a great introduction to printing. Using a few basic supplies, you can create personalized objects for the home and beyond. Once you have tried this idea, play with shape, scale and colour to make your own bespoke creations.

1.

Draw Motifs
Interpret the seasons by drawing four simple motifs – clouds for autumn, raindrops for winter, sunshine for summer and grass for spring. When you are happy with your designs, cut out the templates.

MATERIALS

Pencil and paper.

Scissors or craft knife.

Craft foam sheets.

Strong glue such as UHU.

Wooden blocks slightly larger than the shapes you want to print.

1m *(39in)* plain fabric, washed, dried and ironed.

Fabric inks.

Large spoon.

Rubber roller and palette.

Old towel.

Sewing machine.

General Knowledge
When working with fabric ink, choose a tightly woven fabric to ensure the ink does not seep through. The colour of the fabric will have an impact on how the ink colour appears.

Expand your printing repertoire by trying out stencil printing, lino printing or printing with found objects.

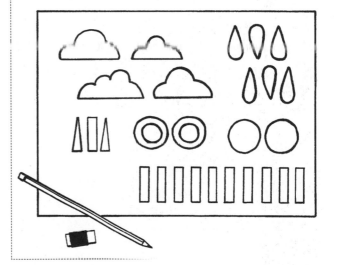

2.

Cut and Stick the Foam
Draw around the templates on to the foam and cut out. Gently stick the foam shapes to the wooden blocks using strong glue, and leave to dry.

3.

Prepare Fabric
Cut the fabric into four pieces, each 42cm *(16½in)* square. Keep the remaining fabric for test printing.

4.

Prepare Inks and Test Print
Mix the inks well to avoid streaks. Place two spoonfuls of ink on the palette. Run the roller back and forth through the ink to ensure that it is evenly covered. Place an old towel on a level table to give some resistance when printing.

Put the scrap fabric on the table. With the roller, gently roll over one of the blocks, coating it evenly. Be careful not to get any ink around the design and on the wood. Gently lower the inked block and press it firmly, keeping it flat. Raise the stamp and check your test print. If the ink is spreading out of the design, there is too much ink; if it is too faint, there isn't enough or you are not applying enough pressure. Repeat until you are happy with the prints. Note how much ink and pressure you apply for an accurate print.

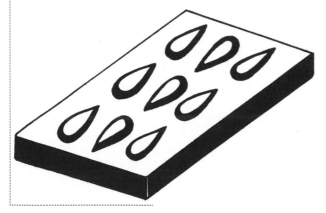

5.

Print

Place a square of fabric on the table and print a napkin, working from side to side in a straight row. Once one row is completed, move down to the next and continue the process until the napkin is covered. Pay attention to the block, maintaining the amount of ink and checking that it is clean around the foam design.

When you have finished with your first motif, clean the stamp and roller. Repeat the printing process until you have printed all four napkins. Let them dry fully and then iron with a high heat setting to make the print permanent.

6.

Finish Edges

With the fabric print side down, fold over 5mm (³⁄₁₆in) on each edge and press, then repeat. Secure with pins then sew a running stitch along all four hems, removing the pins as you go.

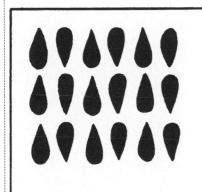

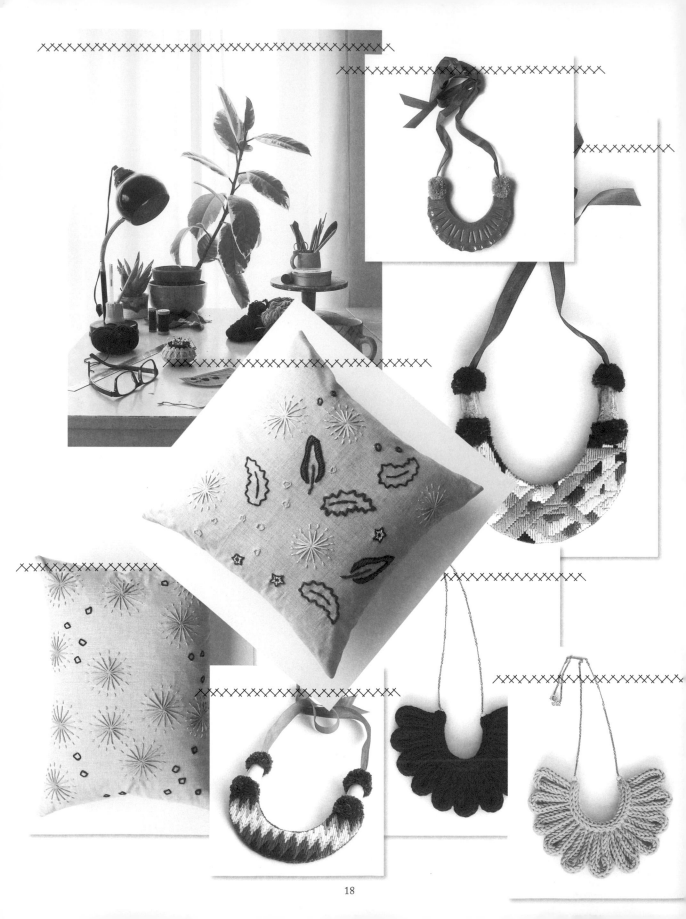

Anna Alicia

A. Alicia

Anna Alicia's work is always changing; her ethical approach to making, using ecologically friendly materials to ensure her product is sustainable, means that her designs are very materials-led. Anna engages with the process of crafting, striving to understand how things work and what potential results could be. This approach has enabled her to work with knitting, embroidery and ceramics, among other techniques. Although her choice of resources dictates what she does somewhat, Anna's work manages to be cohesive as well as varied.

Anna has experience of working both in a studio space and from home. She recognizes the need for a space to create, and the importance of maintaining a balance between work and life. One constant in her space is the need for light, supporting her need to be surrounded by plants.

Anna forgoes sketching for the excitement of experimenting directly with materials and processes. From this evolve her designs for textile- and ceramic-based jewellery and accessories, which she sells online. Colour plays a key role in Anna's work. She draws inspiration from natural forms and the way that artists work with hue and tone. This is then applied to her pieces, in which she tries out colour combinations and textures to interpret the environment: wood, mountains, flora and fauna.

Anna believes in the importance of lifelong learning, and runs workshops to share her stitching skills. In this way she encourages adults to relinquish their fear of making mistakes for the pleasure of experimenting with fabric and yarn. Anna has extended this approach in her book *Make it Your Own*, in which she seeks to share how, with simple, portable techniques, people can apply their own design style to the home.

From her plant-filled workspace, Anna Alicia's stitched work shows
natural forms reimagined in jewellery and home accessories.

Bargello
Embroidery
Collar

ANNA
ALICIA

The Bargello style is named after the upholstery featured on a group of seventeenth-century chairs at the Bargello Palace in Florence; it is also known by other names, including Florentine stitch. The technique uses a series of stepped vertical stitches to create a geometric pattern. The process of choosing colour and the repetition involved in creating this project make it very satisfying. Preparation is essential to ensure the collar pieces match.

MATERIALS

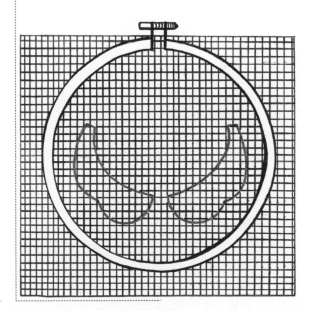

Template and stitching chart from CD.

Interlock embroidery canvas, 50 x 50cm *(19⅝ x 19⅝in)*, 14hpi.

30cm *(12in)* embroidery hoop.

Debbie Bliss Eco Baby yarn (or a similar 'baby' or 'sports' weight wool) in a range of colours.

Crewel or tapestry needle.

Eco-felt in one of your wool colours, 30 x 30cm *(12 x 12in)*.

Grosgrain ribbon, 1m long *(39in)* x 1cm *(⅜in)* wide, to suit your wool colours.

Cotton thread to match the felt.

Sharp hand-sewing needle.

Decorative button (optional).

1.
Prepare Template and Canvas

Cut out the template for one side of the collar. Stretch the canvas over the embroidery hoop. Lay the template on the right-hand side of the canvas, and draw round it in pencil.

Turn the template over and draw round it again on the other half of the canvas, making sure there is at least 2cm *(¾in)* between the outlines. If you want the two collar panels to be exactly the same, make sure you line them up as an exact mirror image on the grid of the canvas.

General Knowledge
To mirror shapes successfully, find the centre-point of the canvas and draw a horizontal line. Working in this way will also enable you to create other shapes and your own accessory designs.

This kind of needlework is usually done with tapestry wool. This can give a traditional feel to your work and suits pastoral motifs, which can demand muted tones.

2.

Stitch

With the wool and the crewel needle, embroider one panel first then mirror the stitching on the other panel. Thread the needle with a length of wool and knot the end. To form a zigzag pattern, bring the needle through from the back on the left-hand side of one of the outlines. Count five threads up from where you started and take the needle through to the back (if this takes you outside the pencil marks, just take the needle back through the last hole within the outline instead: always keep inside it). Now move one thread to the right and two threads up from the bottom of the first stitch, and make a stitch the same length as before. Repeat this with two more stitches, moving across one thread and up two threads each time.

After four stitches, start coming down by two threads with each stitch until you are level with your first stitch, then start working upwards again.

Keep repeating the pattern until you reach the other edge of the outline. Stitch a knot on the back of the embroidery and cut the remaining wool.

Change the wool colour and start the next row of stitches four threads below the first. Bring the needle from the back to the front, then take it back through the hole at the bottom of the stitch above (so both stitches share the hole). Continue in this way, keeping the stitches the same length (four holes in this example) so that they follow the zigzag of the first row.

Build up rows of different colours and different-length stitches (between four- and seven-hole stitches work best) until the outline is completely filled in.

Mirror the stitches on the other outline.

3.

Cut around Canvas

Remove the canvas from the hoop and cut around the embroidered panels 1cm *(⅜in)* from their edges. Snip into the canvas border at roughly 1.5cm *(½in)* intervals, then fold the canvas under the embroidery.

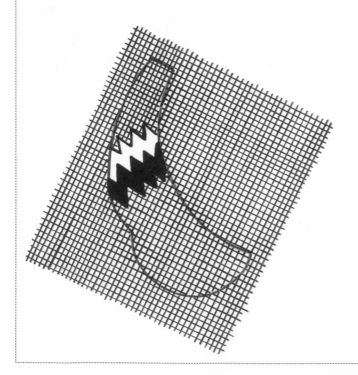

4.

Cut Felt
Lay the embroidered shapes on the felt, pin in place and cut the felt to size (it should be exactly the same size as the embroidered panels).

5.

Attach Ribbon
Cut two lengths of ribbon, 50cm *(19⅝in)* each. Poke about 2cm *(¾in)* of one end of each piece between the felt and the embroidered canvas at the top of each panel, pin and stitch in place.

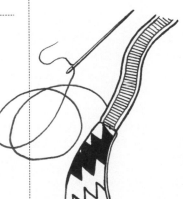

6.

Add Wool to Edge
Take a length of wool and similarly poke the end between the canvas and the felt, next to the ribbon. Stitch in place. Run the wool around the edge, along the join between the embroidered canvas and the felt, over-sewing it in place as you go. When you get all the way round, tuck the end of the wool in and sew in place. Repeat with the other embroidered panel. This should hold the embroidery to the felt, and the wool will help to cover the seam between the two.

7.

Sew Panels Together
Sew the two panels together at their tips to form the collar. You could also add a button here for decoration if you wanted.

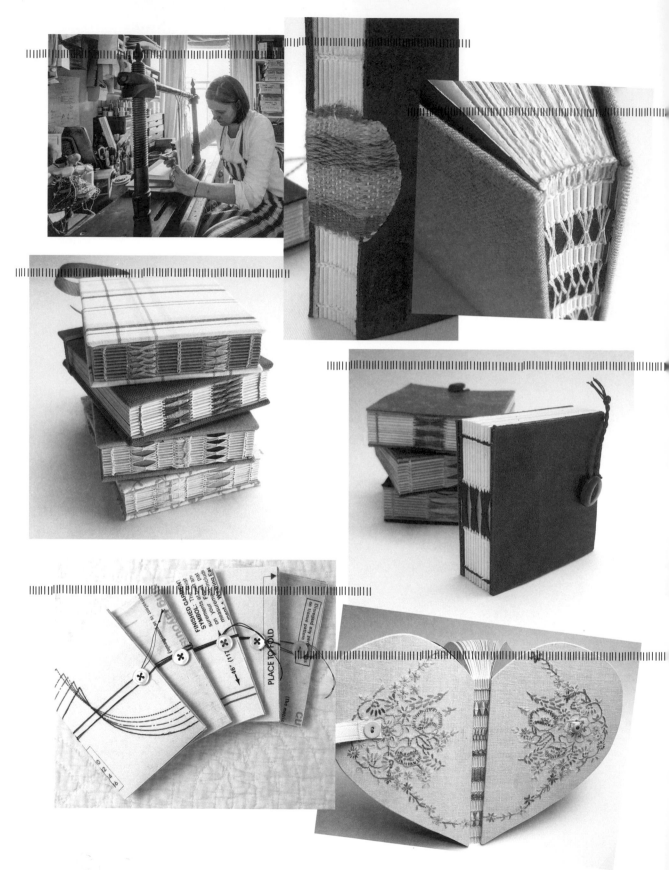

Kate Bowles

Artist and Craft Maker

Kate Bowles is an artist who makes books. With her dedication to lifelong learning and her belief that it is one's obligation to pass on real skills, Kate finds her work varied and challenging, and a satisfying occupation.

The books Kate creates feature an open spine, highlighting the stitches by leaving the spine exposed. Having first encountered this technique in the work of the artist and bookbinder Sarah Brown, Kate attended a workshop and learned how to make her own book from start to finish. This experience drove her to pursue further binding methods, adding to her repertoire and learning more about the history of the process.

Tied into the history of book-making is the marginalization of women in the bindery. In Victorian times, women were limited to carrying out a narrow range of tasks with few tools. With a long-standing interest in the reclamation and recognition of female arts, and the Art versus Craft debate, Kate has made her practice much more than a one-dimensional pastime. Her use of exposed stitching and her vibrant style are a nod to the women of the nineteenth-century binderies.

Kate works with found haberdashery items and discarded materials, and so her ideas are dictated by the resources she seeks to repurpose. Her intention is to give greater worth to items with a low perceived value and status. Kate dyes her own linen thread using natural processes, employing the advice of natural dye artist Claire Wellesley-Smith. The books are designed to be functional and made to be used, in line with Kate's principle of recycling and developing creative skills.

By employing traditional apparatus, techniques and stitches, Kate Bowles repurposes old items into tactile journals and albums.

Hand-Bound Notebook

KATE BOWLES

Creating a book is hugely gratifying. Employing a variety of skills and requiring patience and precision, this project provides a satisfying challenge. Learning the language of bookbinding, including new stitch terms, enriches the experience further, enabling the sewist to engage with a craft that is steeped in history. This project makes a book measuring 9.5 x 9.5cm *(3¼ x 3¼in)*.

MATERIALS

Assorted paper, at least 63 sheets, 18 x 9cm *(7⅛ x 3½in)*

Bone folder.

Waste paper.

Self-adhesive linen tape.

2 sheets coloured paper, 2cm *(¾in)* wider than the paper sheets.

PVA glue and paste brush.

Clean rag.

Bookbinding press or heavy books.

Craft knife, metal ruler and cutting board.

1 ribbon 1 x 70cm *(⅜ x 27⅝in)*.

2 ribbons 1 x 40cm *(⅜ x 15¾in)*.

Awl.

Linen thread.

Beeswax block.

Masking tape.

Bookbinding needle.

Double-sided tape (optional).

2mm *(³⁄₃₂in)* grey board.

Book cloth or fabric.

Waste card (such as a cereal packet).

1.

Create Signatures
Create 63 folios (folded pages) using the bone folder. The paper should be cut so that the grain runs from the top of the page to the bottom. Group together six folios to make a signature; you will need ten signatures in total. You will have three folios left over to make two end-pages and a template for the sewing holes.

2.

End-Pages

The paper attached to the book cover needs to be reinforced with linen to prevent it from tearing. Take an A4 sheet of waste paper and lay two of the leftover folios open on it. Position the linen tape over the fold in the middle of each folio, then lift it and stick it down.

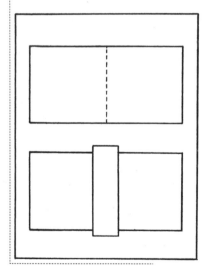

3.

Add Coloured Paper

Place one of the coloured pieces of paper on a waste piece of paper and cover with a thin layer of PVA. Position the coloured paper on one side of the end-page folio, ensuring that it overlaps the linen tape by about 4mm *(⁵⁄₃₂in)*. Make sure there are no air bubbles by smoothing the paper down with a clean rag. Repeat with the second end-page, then cover both with a clean piece of waste paper and pop into a press or heavy book until dry (about an hour).

Remove the end-papers from the press or heavy book. Remove the waste paper by sliding the bone folder between the two layers, and trim off the excess coloured paper using a craft knife and metal ruler.

Using the bone folder, score along the original crease and fold the end-paper so that the linen tape is on the outside edge. Add the end-pages to the book block with the coloured pages on the inside. Mark the book block by writing 'front' and 'back' on the relevant pages.

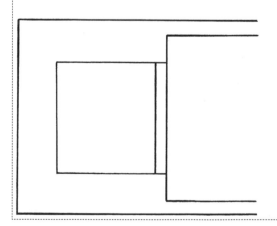

4.

Make Template for Sewing Holes

Take the remaining folio and make a pencil mark 5mm *(³⁄₁₆in)* in from either end of the folded edge (this is for the kettle stitches). Make a light mark at the centre of the folio. Place the longest ribbon on the centre point and mark 1mm *(¹⁄₃₂in)* to either side of it. Place the shorter ribbons either side of the middle ribbon, and make marks as before.

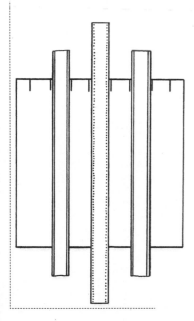

5.

Make Sewing Holes

Take the front page and open it up so that the folded edge is on the edge of the table or a book. Place the template against the fold, making sure the edges line up. With the awl at a 45-degree angle, make a hole through the fold where you have marked the template (making sure your other hand is out of the way, to avoid injury). Repeat this process for all the signatures. The book block will now be in reverse, with the back page on top.

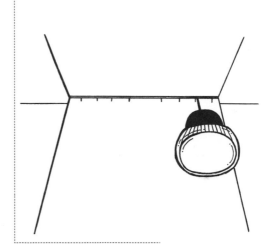

6.

Add Ribbons

Wax the linen thread by running it through the beeswax block from the centre of the piece of thread to one end, then from the centre to the other end. This will protect the thread from the paper and prevent it from fraying.

Line the ribbons up with the first folio, and make sure the plain side, marked 'back', is face down. Secure the ribbons with masking tape.

7.

Sew the Book Block 1

Knot the end of the linen thread, leaving a 7.5cm *(3in)* tail. Starting with the right-hand hole, sew in and out of the sewing holes, making sure that the thread does not catch on the ribbons as you sew over them. This is known as long stitch.

8.

Sew the Book Block 2

Place the next signature on top of the first, line up the holes, and sew into the left-hand hole. Sew long stitches to the end of the signature. When you get to the last hole in the signature, make a kettle stitch by running the needle behind the stitch below from right to left and sewing through the loop in the thread. You are now ready to sew into the next signature.

Traditionally, stitches are tightened by hooking the thread under existing threads every third or fourth row. When you have sewn the last signature, remember to do a kettle stitch, then go back into the last hole, wrap the thread around existing threads and knot. Remove the masking tape, then secure the loose end of thread at the bottom of the book in the same way. Attach the ribbons to the book block using glue or double-sided tape.

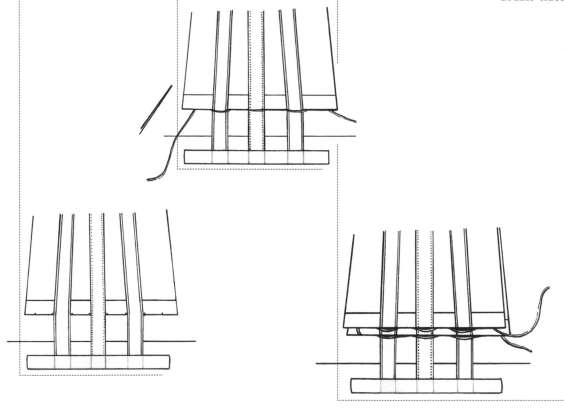

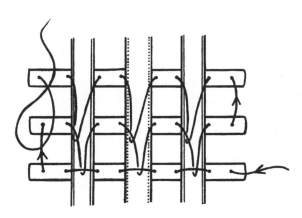

Kettle Stitch

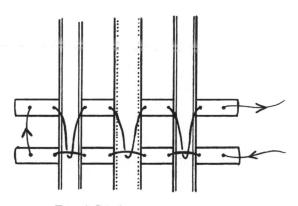

French Stitch

9.

Make the Covers 1

Measure the book and cut two pieces of grey board a few millimetres larger all round. Mark the board to show the direction of the grain. It is very important that the grain of the board runs parallel to the spine of the book.

Place the book cloth face down on a clean piece of waste paper and paste glue in the area that you will place the board. Place the board on the book cloth and press down. Trim the excess cloth as shown, leaving a border of 1.5cm (½in) and making sure there is at least 2mm (⅛in) of extra cloth at the corners. Repeat for the second cover.

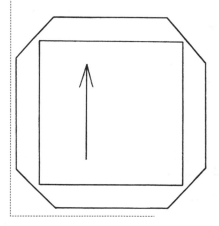

10.

Make the Covers 2

For each cover, glue the top and bottom edges of the cloth and fold over using the waste paper (this will help to keep the cover free of glue). Turn the cover 90 degrees and tuck in the corners with your fingernail. Glue the edge and fold over as before. The moisture in the glue will cause the covers to warp, so you need to work quickly. If you are covering the book with normal cloth, you will get a cleaner finish by using double-sided tape.

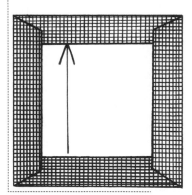

11.

Attach Covers

Place a piece of waste paper behind the page you wish to glue, to protect the book block. Put a thin layer of glue on the cover, then a thin layer on the front page and ribbons. Position the cover and press down. Ensure the cover is attached by opening the book and rubbing the page with a clean rag to smooth out any bubbles. Paste the inside of the end-page and attach to cover, rubbing with a rag again. Place a piece of waste card between the newly glued pages and the book block to prevent moisture from warping the non-glued pages. Turn the book over and repeat with the back cover. Place in a bookbinding press or under heavy books and leave until dry (2–3 hours).

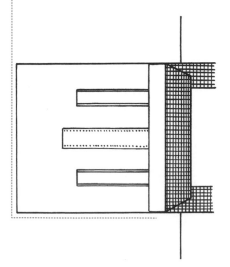

General Knowledge
When preparing to sew the book block, it is essential to line up the holes. Take time to line up each folio with the template. When you have made the holes, line up the signatures to check that they match before you start to sew.

Sewing the signatures together needs to be approached with care. The beeswax will help to prevent the paper from tearing, but be sure not to pull the thread too hard.

While sewing, keep the ribbon taut – this will help to maintain the structure and firmness of the book block.

Abigail Brown

Artist and Craft Maker

Abigail Brown's library of textile birds is testament to her approach to her work, reflecting careful research, pattern design and an intense process of making. Drawing from her collection of colour-categorized boxes of fabric, Abigail employs her understanding of hue, texture and pattern to replicate nature in cloth sculpture. Detail is vital, and it is applied with tiny hand stitches, showing the delicate nature of both Abigail's work and the birds themselves.

Operating from a shared studio, Abigail enjoys the camaraderie that comes with working among other makers. She occasionally needs to employ extra help; however, her small space lends itself to her compact projects and the display of a small selection of her creations, such as the papier-maché animal heads that adorn her wall.

Abigail works with great diligence, but takes the time to connect with her followers through intimate workshops, which she conducts in her studio. She enjoys imparting her experience and seeing how the attendees take her techniques and ideas and make them their own. However, Abigail is mindful of the need to protect her ideas; having spent years developing her style and method, she is keen to share but not to be replicated.

Keenly influenced by her grandmother, an expert seamstress, Abigail has been enthusiastic about fabric and stitching from an early age, and it is this devotion that drives her work. In keeping with working with fragments of fabric, Abigail has also employed scraps of paper to form a series of animal sculptures, developing her work into a mythical menagerie. By working with new materials, she can develop her own skills and produce bigger pieces in a shorter time.

Careful concentration and delicate work see Abigail Brown's detailed menagerie come to life in her London studio.

Cat
Doll

ABIGAIL
BROWN

This sedate doll is a pleasure to create. The process of construction, forming the limbs, hand stitching the facial features and finally dressing the doll is wonderfully gratifying. Choose well-worn fabrics or raid your scrap box to make a doll with personal meaning.

MATERIALS

◎ Templates from CD, cut out with a 1cm (⅜in) seam allowance.

Calico for main body, head, arms and legs, approx. 60cm (23⅝in) square.

Pencil or fabric pen.

Small amount of grey fabric for face.

Iron-on transfer adhesive.

Thread in various colours: white, black, grey and pink.

Sewing machine.

Small amounts of pink fabric for ears, cheeks and bracelet.

Small amount of light brown fabric for feet.

Polyester stuffing.

Tiny bell or bead for bracelet (optional).

45 x 14cm (17¾ x 5½in) black spotty fabric for collar/ruff, or fabric of your choice.

1.

Cut Out the Head

Using the template, cut out two identical pieces from the calico for the head, including the seam allowance of 1cm (⅜in). Transfer the relevant markings to the fabric pieces using pencil or fabric pen.

Cut a rectangle 10 x 6cm (4 x 2⅜in) from the grey fabric, and a piece of iron-on transfer adhesive, with the backing paper, to the same size. Iron the adhesive glue side down to the wrong side of the fabric until the glue is melted and firmly set. Cut out a triangle to sit as shown by the thin blue lines on the template. Iron in place.

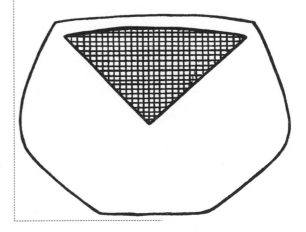

2.

Sew the Head

Place the piece face side down and mark with a pencil dot where the point of the triangle sits. Fold the face in half, right sides together, and make a dot 1cm *(³⁄₈in)* from the centre line at top of the head. Connect the two dots with a pencil line. Use the sewing machine to sew down this pencil line, creating a dart.

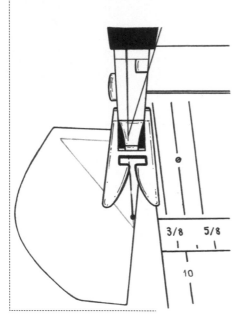

3.

Complete the Head

Cut the edge off close to the stitched line. Repeat with the plain back piece. Place the two pieces on top of each other, insides touching, seamed sides out, and pin in place.

Machine stitch around the head, leaving gaps where dotted lines appear on the template. Cut slits into the hem of the curved areas of the face, not too close to the stitch line. Turn inside out.

4.

Make the Body

Using the template, cut out two identical pieces from the calico for the body, remembering to include a 1cm *(³⁄₈in)* seam allowance. Transfer the relevant markings to the pattern pieces using pencil or fabric pen.

Pin the body pieces together, right sides facing, and sew, leaving gaps where dotted lines appear on the template. Trim the stitched corners and turn inside out. Iron.

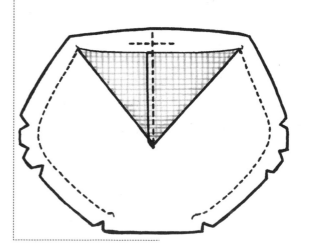

5.

Make the Ears

Using the ear template, trace and cut out two pieces from the calico, including a 1cm *(⅜in)* seam allowance. For each ear, cut a piece of pink fabric to the same size.

Pin the two pieces right sides together and sew, leaving the dotted line as an open edge. Trim seams close to the stitch line and turn inside out. Iron.

6.

Make the Arms

Draw round the arm template twice, then turn it over and draw round it twice more to create two pieces in mirror image. For each arm, pin and sew two pieces of calico right sides together, avoiding the dotted line. Trim the seams close to the stitch line, and turn inside out. Iron.

7.

Make the Legs

Cut out four rectangles from the calico, each 20 x 5cm *(7⅞ x 2in)*. Cut out four smaller rectangles from the light brown fabric, each 5cm *(2in)* square. Take one piece of calico and lay a piece of brown on top at one end, as shown. Pin in place and sew a line along the bottom, 5mm *(⁄₁₆in)* from the edge. Press the seam open. Repeat with each piece of calico.

Take two pieces and lay them on top of each other, seam sides out. Pin in place. Draw round the leg template with a 5mm *(⁄₁₆in)* seam allowance, pin and sew, avoiding the dotted line. Repeat with the second leg. Trim the seams close to the stitch line and turn inside out.

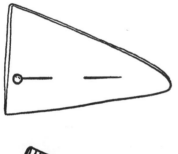

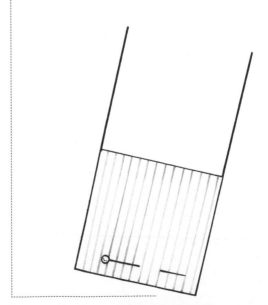

8.

Sew Together and Stuff

Take the head and the ears. Insert the left ear a little way into the ear hole, pink side forward, and sew into position by hand. Repeat with the right ear. Stuff the head.

Fold the neck seam in so the edges are hidden. Insert the top of the body piece a little way into the neck hole and sew it into position.

Stuff the two arms and legs, leaving the stuffing ends open. One by one, put the arms into the armholes and sew in position.

Turn the open bottom of the body in so the edges aren't showing, creating a neat line. Position the left leg a little way into the opening, against the left side, and sew into position. Use the remaining gap to stuff the body, then insert the right leg a little way into the gap and sew it into position.

9.

Create the Face

Cut a piece of calico 5 x 5cm *(2 x 2in)*, and a piece of pink and a piece of brown fabric 4cm *(1⅝in)* square. Cut out pieces from the iron-on transfer adhesive to match. Iron the adhesive to the fabric.

Cut the transfer-backed calico into two rectangles and place them on top of each other, glue side out. Cut two oval shapes for the eyes, slightly feathered at the ends, so they are mirrors of each other when opened.

Cut out two small circles from the pink. Cut out two small ovals from the brown. Arrange the pink cheeks and the white eye pieces on the face, glue side down, and gently use the iron to set the glue. Now place the brown

pieces on the white ones and set with the iron again.

Use a pencil to draw the oval eye shape in the brown and use as a guide to stitch in the black of the eye. Use black thread to sew the nose and the little black specks on either side. Use grey thread to sew lines up the grey fabric section. Use pink thread to add detail to the ears and cheeks, if you wish.

10.

Make the Bracelet

Cut a strip of pink fabric about 1 x 10cm *(⅜ x 4in)*. Tie it round the wrist in one little knot. Stitch in the little bell or bead if you have one; this will also secure the fabric. Stitch it simply in place if you don't have a bell or bead to add.

11.

Make the Collar

Cut a strip of the collar fabric 45 x 14cm *(17¾ x 5½in)*. Fold it in half and machine stitch the ends as shown.

Turn the right way out and, taking a length of doubled black thread, hand sew a running stitch along the folded edge all the way round, keeping the needle and thread in place when you finish.

Pull the collar up over the cat's body and arms to sit in place around the neck. Pull the thread tight to create the ruffled effect, until it can't be pulled any further, and knot or stitch the end to secure it. Twist the collar round so the seam is hidden at the back.

General Knowledge

The markings on the templates indicate where to sew and where to leave gaps.

When stuffing the doll, use small pieces and work it into the space using a knitting needle for limbs and corners.

Turning the limbs can take time. Use a safety pin secured to the sewn tip to pull the fabric right side out.

When hand sewing, use a doubled thread and tiny running stitches.

Katie Wagstaff

Oh Squirrel

At the centre of Katie Wagstaff's work is the intention to raise a smile. Following years of collecting, Katie created the stationery brand Oh Squirrel, applying her treasured finds to a range of greetings cards and repurposing old objects in innovative ways. Katie is a mixed-media maker, with sewing at the core of her work. Her papercraft, printing and graphic-design skills all play a part in the overall aesthetic of her label, enabling her to tap into many different crafts and styles, and fuelling new products and collections.

Creating a dialogue between herself and her customers is essential to Katie's work. Her regular presence at independent markets allows her to meet her buyers and to see what makes people tick. Katie's work evokes a sense of optimism befitting the cards and paraphernalia that belong to a celebration. She also works to commission, relying on both her design skills and her ability to collaborate with her clients on a personal level.

Having grown up in an environment where crafting was an everyday occupation, Katie defers to her mother if sewing dilemmas arise, honouring the tradition of handmade skills being passed down through generations. Katie's knowledge of textiles, acquired through her training as a fashion designer, informs her creations. In her home studio she practises techniques of fabric manipulation using natural colouring and washes and an abundance of tea-dyeing.

Although Katie's work is cohesive, it also has an air of eclecticism, perhaps as a result of the drawing together of so many elements and found objects. Her ideas grow from scribbled notes and drawings to become carefully planned and realized articles that exhibit a strong artistic vision.

Surrounded by items and images from the past, Katie Wagstaff shares her preserved collections through her stationery brand.

Sewn Greetings Card

KATIE WAGSTAFF

Happy Birthday

Happy Birthday!

Sewing with paper is very similar to stitching fabric, but – just as there are many different kinds of cloth – card and paper vary in quality and weight. You do not need a special kind of machine or any additional equipment to sew paper. A handmade card makes a prized keepsake for a special occasion.

1.

Prepare the Card
Score the piece of cardboard down the centre to form the basic card structure.

Work out where the photograph will fit best, and secure the fabric to the front of the card using a little double-sided tape. Make sure the tape is central so that you don't sew over it.

MATERIALS

A5 piece of patterned cardboard, approx. 300gsm.

Card scorer (optional).

Photograph, approx. 7 x 11cm *(2¾ x 4⅜in)*.

Piece of fabric approx. 5mm *(³⁄₁₆in)* larger on all sides than the photograph you are using. Recommended fabrics are polycotton, cotton poplin or similar medium-weight cloth with a plain weave.

Double-sided tape.

Sewing machine.

Teflon sewing-machine foot (optional).

Scissors for both paper and fabric.

Stamp and ink pad.

Piece of contrasting paper.

A5 piece of paper.

Corner cutter (optional).

Envelope.

General Knowledge
To check how your sewing machine behaves with paper and card, sew some practice lengths before making the card.

As stitching through cardboard may blunt your needle, use a different needle for paper-based sewing.

A Teflon foot has a base that is treated to enable paper and fabric to pass smoothly through the sewing machine.

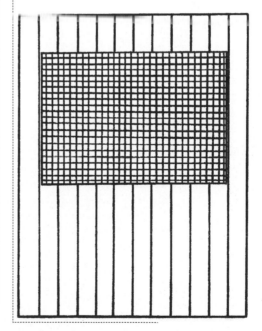

2.

Sew the Fabric
Use the sewing machine on a simple running stitch setting to sew around the edge of the fabric. Reverse the direction to secure your stitches at the beginning and end.

3.

Add Photograph and Sew
Place the photograph on the middle of the fabric, so that it is framed by the fabric. Again, you can use double-sided tape to fix the photograph in place while you sew.

   Using a small zigzag stitch, carefully stitch around the photograph. Trim all loose threads.

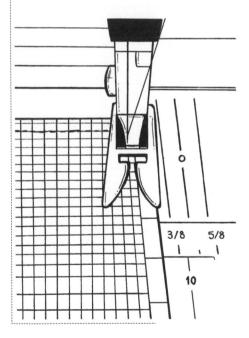

4.

Stamp Greeting
Stamp any words you wish to add on a piece of contrasting paper, and stick to the card using double-sided tape.

5.

Make Insert and Finish
Inside the card, place a length of double-sided tape along the scored line. Score the A5 piece of paper, which will form the insert for your card, and stick it to the tape.

For a professional finish, use a corner cutter to shape the corners of the card.

Kirsty Southam

Me Plus Molly

Kirsty Southam, working under the label Me Plus Molly, is a mixed-media artist. Having acquired the habit of keeping sketchbooks throughout her studies, she documents her work in journals, translating her ideas from the page to three-dimensional objects. Kirsty sells her ready-made projects through markets and Etsy, and encourages others to make with carefully constructed crafting kits.

Originally, Kirsty drew and painted, slowly discovering the potential of textiles, appreciating the tactile nature of fabric and thread and the ability to draw and paint with a needle. There is a distinct flow to her designs, reflecting the way she makes, letting the pattern grow on the fabric as she sews. Kirsty's work features spaces of abstract colour, shape and pattern as well as pictorial elements.

Journalling, both on paper and on screen through her blog, is paramount in Kirsty's work. The act of creating the actual journal within which to experiment is also key; various papers and colours form the environment in which she documents her ideas, making the process organic and tactile, and a springboard for her textile objects. The journals act as a reference, providing inspiration for current products and a reliable source of visual information to inspire new ideas. Kirsty values the insight into the work of others that can be gained through the blogging community, appreciating how others work and inviting readers to engage with her portfolio.

Kirsty is aware of the importance of reusing and recycling materials, and she sources fabric from local charity shops and donations from friends. She works with what she has, forcing herself to be inventive and adapt the materials at hand to her needs. She also favours independent online retailers, who share their fabric finds and supply individual designer-makers, fuelling the desire to create.

Experimentation in textile design, working in paper and cloth –
Kirsty Southam's workspace is a hive of creative activity.

Doodle
Clutch
Purse

KIRSTY SOUTHAM

Kirsty's design is inspired by the pages of her journals, with their collaged layers of paper, paint, pen, ink, tape and doodles. Her design work is textural, decorative and abstract in its look rather than depicting a recognizable image or theme. When working on your purse, let the pattern grow, reflecting your taste and interests.

MATERIALS

Purse frame.

Brown paper.

2 pieces of cotton calico, each 35cm *(13¾in)* square.

Fabric scraps.

Prints or drawings for inspiration.

Fabric pen.

Iron-on transfer paper (optional).

Sewing machine.

2 pieces lining fabric, each 35cm *(13¾in)* square.

2 pieces heavy sew-in interlining, each 35cm *(13¾in)* square.

2 pieces medium/firm fusible interlining, each 35cm *(13¾in)* square.

Blind-stitch sole foot.

Strong textile glue.

1.

Make the Pattern
Lay the purse frame flat on a piece of brown paper, draw around the outside of the frame and mark where the hinges end.

Design your purse pattern around the frame outline you have drawn. Aim to make the angles wider than the frame, and add a seam allowance of 1cm *(⅜in)* to make the purse shape quite full. Make sure the shape you draw is symmetrical.

It is important to mark correctly the position of the purse hinges on the fabric, so the purse will open and close properly. Place the top corner of the purse frame on the top corner of the drawn pattern, line it up with the side of the pattern and make a mark at the hinge end.

Once you are happy with the pattern, cut it out.

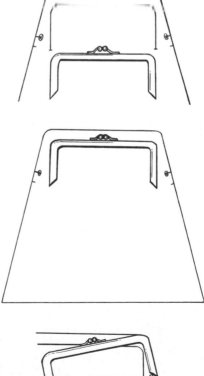

2.

Create the Design

Place the purse pattern on the base fabric and draw around it in pencil. Create your design within this shape. Lay out prints and snippets of fabric and draw lines of stitch in fabric pen. Remember to bear in mind the 1cm *(3/8in)* seam allowance. Sew your design using free machine embroidery.

To create your own printed fabric circles, scan and print images on to transfer paper, cut into circles and iron, then sew on to the purse in the same way as the rest of the design.

Once you have finished stitching both sides, cut the purse out and press.

3.

Sew Purse

Using the paper pattern, cut two pieces of lining fabric, two of heavy sew-in interlining and two of fusible interlining. Iron the fusible interlining to the reverse of the outside fabric design, starting in the middle and working outwards. If you have used transfer paper, lay a piece of baking paper down first to avoid sticking the design to the ironing board.

Create a sandwich of the outside fabric (right sides together) and then the sew-in interlining on top and bottom. Pin everything together and use the pattern to mark where the hinges are.

Starting from one hinge mark, sew along the side and bottom leaving a 1cm *(3/8in)* seam allowance, finishing at the other hinge mark.

Make a flat bottom by taking a corner of the purse, matching the side seam with the bottom seam, flattening it, measuring between 3cm *(1 1/8in)* and 4cm *(1 5/8in)* from the end and stitching across the corner. Trim the excess fabric. Repeat for the other side. Turn the purse right side out.

Sew the lining fabric as you did the outside, but this time leave an opening in the bottom of the lining to pull the whole purse through. Create a flat bottom to the lining in the same way as for the outside purse. Put the outside purse into the lining, with right sides facing.

Pin one of the flap sides together and stitch from hinge mark to hinge mark; repeat with the other side. Pull the outside purse through the opening in the lining, push the lining into the purse, smooth everything and press.

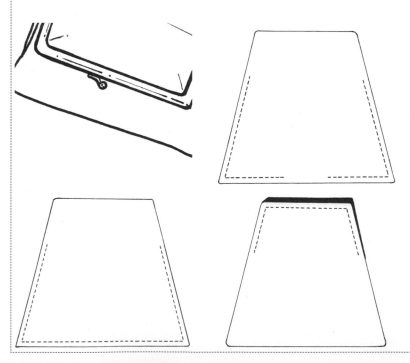

4.

Secure the Hinges

After ironing, to combat any small gaps that may appear near the hinges, use a blind-stitch sole foot with the needle set slightly to the left to stitch from the middle of the top of one flap (over the hinges) right back round to your original starting point.

Sew the gap in the lining closed either by hand or by machine.

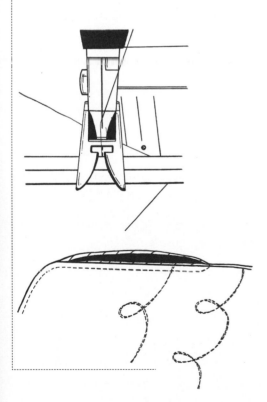

5.

Attach Purse to Frame

Glue the purse into the frame one side at a time. Apply a generous amount of glue to the frame channel. Apply glue to the top edge and sides of the purse. Allow the glue to dry for at least four minutes, so that it is tacky rather than wet.

Insert the purse into the frame, top edge first and then the hinge ends. Use a small, sharp pair of sewing scissors or similar to help you push it into the frame. Make sure the purse is inserted on all sides. Leave the frame to dry for at least 15 minutes before gluing the other side. Let it dry for a while, then pick off any bits of stray glue.

General Knowledge

If you have never used a blind-stitch sole foot before, try it out on a scrap of fabric before sewing your purse.

Experiment with purse shapes. Make a toile to test out your designs before cutting out your best fabric. Once you have designed a successful pattern, make a copy and keep it for future reference.

Leanne Sarah Smith

Bobbin & Bumble

Leanne Sarah Smith grew up in a family that practised a wealth of art and textile techniques. She immersed herself in the extensive knowledge afforded her from an early age, learning a variety of hand-embroidery stitches from her mother and using them to embellish her dolls' clothes. Surrounded by so much knowledge, Leanne gathered the rudiments of sewing, and an ability to handle the practical functions of the craft, but took more time to realize the creative potential of the sewing machine. It was through discovering free machine embroidery that she found she could combine her passion for drawing with her sewing skills.

Fascinated by the potential of working in textiles, Leanne constantly hones her skills, drawing inspiration from her surroundings and a wealth of artists and makers, including the detailed sewn works of Jazmín Berakha and the highly influential William Morris.

Leanne started her business, which focuses on creating modern, interesting home accessories, in response to requests from her peers for original handmade pieces. Taking tentative steps into selling to a wider audience, Leanne now sells online and through markets where she can meet other designer-makers and communicate with her buyers personally. Her intention is to keep Bobbin & Bumble handmade. She attaches great importance to the connection between the maker, the product and the buyer. Keen to expand her body of work, Leanne continues to develop her repertoire, stitching a series of wall hangings that employ a combination of hand and machine embroidery. This is testament to her work as an artist, making for the purposes of exhibition and exploration of her craft.

In Leanne Sarah Smith's studio, larger exhibition works in progress sit among pieces for sale created with great attention to detail.

Bee Appliqué Cushion

LEANNE SARAH SMITH

Essentially, appliqué involves applying fabric to a larger fabric base. This cushion uses machine embroidery to make a bold and original design. It calls for a fabric that is heavy enough to take the dense stitching, such as wool or a heavy linen or cotton. For the appliqué, choose cotton or another fabric that doesn't fray easily.

MATERIALS

Pattern paper.

2 pieces main fabric for the cushion, 50cm *(19⅝in)* square (use different fabrics if you prefer a contrasting back).

Tailor's chalk.

Fabric scissors (large and small).

Tacking thread and needle.

 Template from CD.

A4 sheet of tracing paper.

HB pencil.

Fabric for appliqué, 50cm *(19⅝in)* square.

Iron-on transfer adhesive, 50cm *(19⅝in)* square.

Fabric stabilizer such as Stitch and Tear, 50cm *(19⅝in)* square.

Fine black pen.

Sewing machine with free machine embroidery foot and invisible zip foot.

Machine embroidery thread.

41cm *(16in)* invisible zip.

40cm *(15¾in)* square cushion pad.

1.

Make a Pattern
Measure out a 41 x 41cm *(16 x 16in)* square on the pattern paper and add a 1cm *(⅜in)* seam allowance on all sides. Cut to size.

Iron the main cushion fabric. Place the pattern on the right side of the fabric, lining it up using the selvedge as a guide and leaving 2.5cm *(1in)* of fabric all round. Pin in place and mark the position with tailor's chalk. Remove the pattern and cut roughly 2.5cm *(1in)* around the outline – this will be cut to size when the appliqué is finished. Repeat for the cushion back, but cut this piece to size.

To help with the placing of the appliqué, mark out a cross-section on the cushion front by finding the centre of the length and width of the piece and joining the opposing points with lines of tacking thread. Put the cushion pieces to one side.

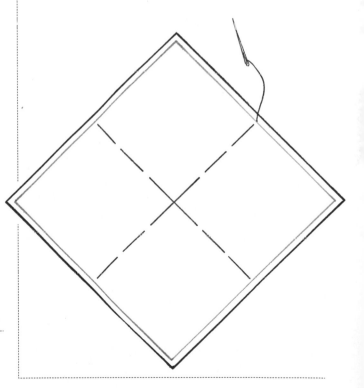

2.

Create Appliqué Pieces

Use the template to trace the bee design on to tracing paper. You need only draw one bee.

Iron the appliqué fabric and cut out a piece of transfer adhesive big enough for four bees. Place the transfer adhesive on to the wrong side of the fabric with the paper side facing up, and iron in place.

Trace four bees on to the paper backing. If you are using a patterned fabric, make sure to consider the placement of the print.

Using a pair of small fabric scissors, cut out each bee 1mm *(¹⁄₃₂in)* outside the traced lines. Carefully peel off the paper backing but do not throw it away, as you will need it later.

3.

Position the Bees

Place one bee on each quarter of the front cushion piece, using the tacked cross-section as a guide. The top of the bee's legs should be 7.5cm *(3in)* from the centre both vertically and horizontally, leaving a gap of 5mm *(³⁄₁₆in)* from the central lines.

Carefully iron the bees in place, then unpick the tacking stitches.

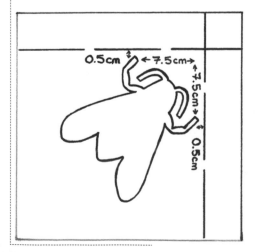

4.

Sew the Bee Detail
To give extra stability to the fabric, cut a piece of Stitch and Tear to the same size as the front cushion fabric, and pin to the wrong side.

Using the paper backing from the transfer adhesive, trace the detail of the bee design in fine black pen on to the opposite side of the pencil drawing. There is no need to draw the outline. Pin the paper bee in place over the corresponding fabric bee, to make a sewing template.

Set the sewing machine up for free machine embroidery. Position the needle where a line starts, feed the fabric through gently, take it slowly and follow the template, ensuring that you secure the stitching by going back and forth at the beginning and end of a line. Avoid going over the same line of stitching twice. Repeat for each bee, cutting off loose threads as you go.

Once all the stitching is done, peel away the paper, using a small pair of scissors or a pin to remove the tricky bits. Add another layer of stitching over the veins of the wings, eyes and stripes of each bee to make them stand out.

5.

Sew the Bee Outline
Change the machine back to normal sewing mode and set the stitching to zigzag. The aim is use satin stitch to pick out the outline of the bees. As machines vary, consult your manual, and do a test on scrap fabric to ensure that you are happy with the stitch.

Taking your time, catch the edge of the appliqué fabric as well as the backing fabric with your stitches. Start with the needle in the fabric, ensuring it is positioned to catch both fabrics. Sew in sections, gently guiding the needle around the shapes. Secure the ends by back stitching, but otherwise do not go back over anywhere you have already stitched. Repeat for each bee.

When all embroidery has been completed, peel off the excess Stitch and Tear from the back of the fabric.

6.

Insert the Zip

Cut the front cushion piece down to match the back. Overlock or zigzag stitch over the raw edges.

Set the machine to a running stitch and attach the invisible zip foot. Place one side of the open zip right side down (teeth facing upwards) on the right side of the fabric, 5mm *(³⁄₁₆in)* from the edge, and pin.

Carefully sew the zip in place, getting as close to the zip teeth as possible. It helps to roll the zip teeth back as you go, and to remove pins before they reach the foot. Reverse stitch at the beginning and end.

Repeat for the other side of the zip, making sure it is positioned on the right side of the fabric. Close the zip to make sure it has been pinned correctly, and unzip before sewing.

7.

Finish the Cushion

Sew the front and back of the cushion together, right sides facing, remembering the 1cm *(³⁄₈in)* seam allowance. Make sure the zip is left open.

On the zip side, sew 5cm *(2in)* in from both edges, then sew down to enclose the zip ends.

Turn the cushion through to the right side, using a blunt-ended implement to turn out the corners. Iron, and insert the cushion pad.

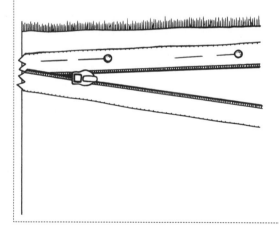

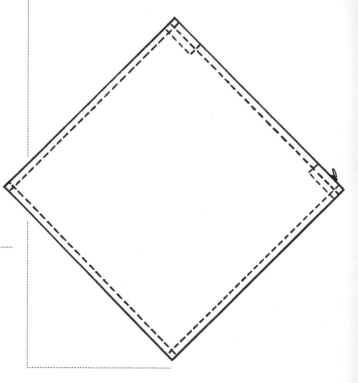

General Knowledge
Not all sewing machines are the same. When trying free machine embroidery, it is important to have the correct foot and to have tested out the settings to make sure the stitch is right.

Free machine embroidery requires concentration. Make sure to sit with a good posture and good lighting, and take breaks if you need them, too.

Hannah Kopacz

Made with Love by Hannah

Hannah Kopacz discovered screen printing at school, choosing the technique not because of its creative potential but for the punk boys who frequented the studio. She developed her skills through a series of jobs ranging from printing to graphic and textile design for the mass market. Her series of roles working for others ended when she united her design and practical skills and took Made with Love by Hannah from a side project to a full-time occupation.

Hannah's home and workspace are packed with collections of kitsch objects and artwork, fabric and trims, which are displayed as a source of constant stimulation. Hannah is a thrift-store enthusiast, and regularly adds to her array of colourful ornaments. Her designs are steeped in a folk style, chosen for its compelling sense of familiarity and a feeling of nostalgia for a time she does not remember but wishes she did. Part of the allure of her work is the hand-crafted nature of the clothing and everyday objects; each carefully made piece stimulates memories of the past.

The outcome of Hannah's reminiscences is a wide range of simply constructed and expertly screen-printed garments, designed and made for women. Keeping a stash of countless sketches, she is never short of inspiration. After making an original drawing, she chooses colours and materials, often dycing the fabric herself before printing. In keeping with her signature style, Hannah's prints are made in an outdoor Alpine-style shack, with the tools of her craft at the centre. Although her print equipment is modern, her expertise as a craftsperson is part of a long history of printmaking.

The imagery in Hannah Kopacz's work echoes folk style and fairytales. Her playful use of colour, executed with precise skill, makes eye-catching and fun garments.

Screen-Printed Mexican-Inspired Apron

HANNAH
KOPACZ

The design of this fun and festive apron is inspired by traditional Mexican Talavera tiles. Screen printing requires practice to perfect, but the results are a great reward. Making this apron shows off your design and is a good opportunity to practise as you create six panels, each printed in two colours.

MATERIALS

Contact paper.

 Design template from CD.

2 screens, approx. 45cm *(17¾in)* square.

Craft knife or scissors.

Textile ink in 3 colours.

Hinge clamps and board.

Scrap fabric.

Spray adhesive (optional).

6 pieces of fabric, each 28cm *(11in)* square.

30cm *(12in)* squeegee.

Sewing machine.

2m *(78¾in)* jumbo ric rac.

Piece of fabric for waistband, 150 x 6cm *(59 x 2⅜in)*.

General Knowledge

The key to successful screen printing is patience. It is easy to get frustrated if your first prints are not perfect, but it takes some time to work out the ideal ink consistency and squeegee pressure for the best prints on different types of material.

1.

Make the Stencil

Cut two pieces of contact paper slightly larger than the inner dimensions of the screen.

Trace the design on to the contact paper, centring it and using a separate piece for each colour. If you want to print the design in a single colour, trace the entire design on to one piece of contact paper.

With a craft knife or scissors, cut out the parts of the design where you want the paint to go.

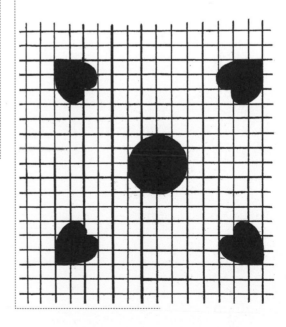

2.

Adhere to Screen
Peel the backing from
the contact paper and
stick it to the flat bottom
of each screen.

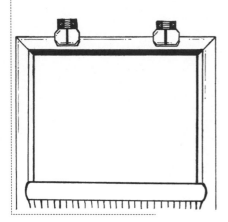

3.

Add Ink
Before handling the ink,
protect your clothing and
your work area.

Use the original
artwork to register the
screen. Place the artwork
on the board, line up the
first screen (red) with the
artwork, and clamp. Mark
the corners of the artwork
on the board and remove
the artwork. You will use
these marks to place the
fabric as you print.

Practise printing on
scrap fabric before using
the project fabric. If you
use a fine film of spray
adhesive on the board to
hold the fabric in place,
it will stay in place if you
make an uneven print and
need to reprint.

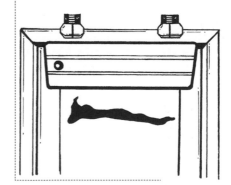

4.

Print

Place the fabric on the board, lining up the corners with the marks on the board. Stir the ink and put a thick line at the top of the screen, above the stencil. Using the squeegee, draw the ink down the screen, making sure it is evenly distributed. If you need to apply more ink, run the squeegee down from top to bottom for a second time.

Print all six pieces with the first colour and allow to dry. Wash the ink out of the screen.

Register the second screen in the same way as the first. Print three pieces with green, wash out the ink and print three pieces with brown. Wash the ink out of the screen.

Iron the prints to heat-set them and make them washable, following the instructions on the ink container.

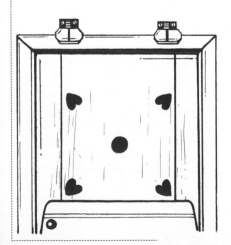

5.

Sew

Lay out the printed pieces in two rows of three. Pin the three vertical sections and sew each section with a 1cm *(⅜in)* seam allowance. Finish the seams with zigzag stitch.

Line up the seams and sew three sections together with the same seam allowance and finish.

Fold the sides and bottom under by 1cm *(⅜in)* and press. Pin the jumbo ric rac around the sides and bottom, and sew.

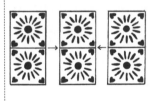

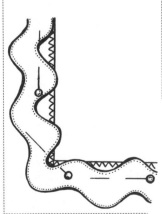

6.

Add Waistband

Sew a long running stitch along the top of the apron, and pull the thread to gather the fabric until it measures 38cm *(15in)* across. Secure the thread with a knot.

Finish all sides of the waistband fabric with zigzag stitch. Press the edges of the waistband under by 1cm *(⅜in)* on all sides. Pin to the apron, lining up the centre of each piece, and sew with a 1cm *(⅜in)* seam allowance.

Sew all around sides of the waistband with a 1cm *(⅜in)* seam allowance.

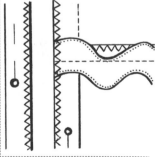

Louise Evans

Felt Mistress

In her home studio, and often in collaboration with her partner, the illustrator Jonathan Edwards, Louise Evans makes creatures in felt and fabric, bringing to life two-dimensional ideas and real-life muses. The malleable nature and sculptural quality of felt make it the perfect material for her extraordinary three-dimensional beings.

Having spent years learning her craft through education and practice at Laura Ashley and in the study of fashion and millinery, Louise has learned the importance of precise stitching and impeccable finish. Well versed in the fit, construction and manufacture of clothing, she is an exceptionally experienced sewist.

The process from first idea to realization is flexible. With the purpose of the final piece in mind, Louise plans both the appearance and the construction, which may include making wire armatures. Once the body is formed, the facial features are pinned on, giving Louise the opportunity to arrive at a design without committing to stitching. Each character she creates has a personality, a back story and carefully chosen clothing and accessories.

Louise enjoys exhibiting her work and contributing to international gallery shows. Her relationship with Gallery Nucleus in Alhambra, California, enables her to make versions of existing characters and to collaborate with other designers, providing a satisfying challenge. Taking pleasure in the positive response of an audience, Louise occasionally teaches creature-making on a small scale, letting people of all ages experience the creative potential of felt and see new and imaginative characters emerge.

With boundless imagination Felt Mistress realizes characters from hand-size creatures to giant fantastical figures in her home studio.

Bertie

LOUISE
EVANS

Sewing with fur, handling the fibres and achieving a consistent look require certain skills. Make Bertie and share in the character-filled world of Felt Mistress, then pay homage by designing your own fur collective.

MATERIALS

 Templates from CD.

Paper.

Tailor's chalk.

35 x 85cm *(13¾ x 33½in)* piece fake fur.

25 x 25cm *(9⅞ x 9⅞in)* grey felt.

Small sharp scissors.

Thread.

Polyester fibre toy stuffing.

Sewing machine.

2 pipe cleaners.

Small pieces of black and white felt for mouth and eyes.

1 pair 16mm *(⅝in)* black plastic safety eyes.

2 x 50g balls of DK yarn for scarf.

4mm *(US 6)* knitting needles.

Crochet hook.

1.

Prepare Pattern Pieces

Cut out the templates from paper. Using tailor's chalk, trace around the paper patterns on to the back of the fake fur and felt, remembering to take note of the direction of the pile when cutting the fur (see arrows on patterns).

Cut around the shapes with sharp scissors. Use shallow cuts when cutting the fur, so that you cut through the backing only, and not the pile.

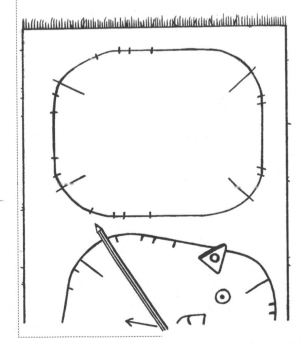

2.

Sew the Limbs

Stitch the bottom furry piece to the bottom of the felt piece, again making sure the direction of the fur pile runs down the limbs. At the bottom fur edge of the limbs, trim away about 4mm *(5/32in)* of fur by pulling back the pile and trimming the layer closest to the bottom edge (don't just trim straight across).

Fold each limb in half with right sides together, and stitch along the longest edge. Repeat with all six limbs. With a chopstick or the points of your scissors, tuck the stray fur fibres into the bottom edge of each limb, and stitch across that bottom edge. Turn the limbs through to the right side. Using a pin, pick out any fur fibres caught in the stitched seams. Stuff all the limbs, leaving a small amount at the top without stuffing, and machine stitch the top edge closed.

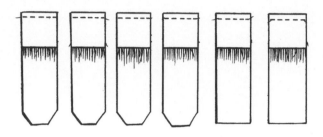

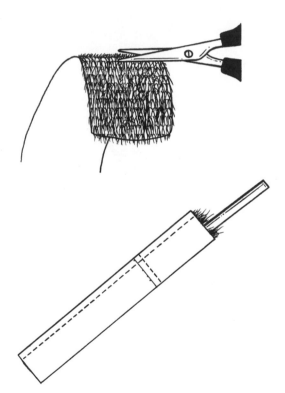

3.

Sew the Antennae

Stitch around the antennae and turn through to the right side. Fold and twist a pipe cleaner in half and insert the folded edge into the antennae. The pipe cleaner should be long enough to stick out of the end of the antennae by about 1cm *(3/8in)*.

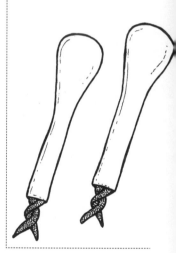

Louise Evans

4.

**Prepare the Body
and Make the Face**
Sew the darts in the
body shapes, tucking any
stray fur fibres in with
scissors as you sew. Make
a hole in the white felt
eye piece and in the front
fur body piece, insert the
plastic safety eye through
both white felt and fur, and
attach the washer to the
back. Hand sew around the
white felt eye piece with a
simple appliqué or over-
sewing stitch.

Stitch the white teeth
to the black mouth shape
using the same hand-
sewing method, then
attach the mouth to the
fur body in the same way.
Once you have stitched the

eyes and mouth in position,
use a pin to release any
caught fur fibres around
these features.

Using the guide marks
from the paper template,
tack all the limbs in
position on the right side
of the front body. Tack
the antennae in the same
way. The sewing machine
should stitch through
the pipe cleaners with no
trouble, but be careful in
case the needle breaks.

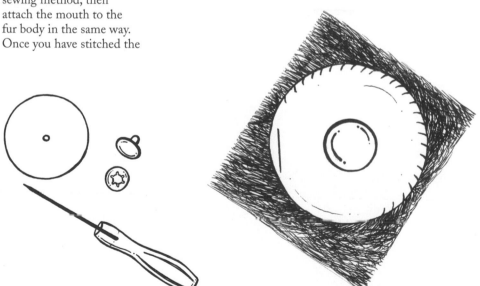

5.

Sew the Body
Put the back body on to the front body with right sides together and stitch around, pushing the fur fibres inwards as you stitch. Remember to leave a gap as marked on the template, for stuffing. You will need to move the limbs, pushing them inside the body as you go around.

6.

Turn and Stuff
Turn the right way out and check all limbs are in the right position and firmly attached. Stuff, using a chopstick or knitting needle to get to all the hard-to-reach areas. Sew up the stuffing gap with strong thread using ladder stitch. Using a pin, go around all the seams, releasing the caught fur fibres. When you have done this, the seams almost become invisible.

Bend the antennae into shape.

7.

Knit the Scarf

Cast on ten stitches and knit in simple garter stitch, changing colour every four rows, until the scarf measures about 85cm *(33½in)*.

   Cut strands of wool 10cm *(4in)* long. Using a crochet hook, fold the wool strands in half and push through the edge of the scarf, then knot. Do this along both edges of the scarf until you have a fringed edge. Trim to neaten.

General Knowledge
If you have attempted to tease out caught fibres with a pin and want to move on to more professional tools, you could invest in a special wire brush for this job from teddy-bear-making supply shops.

✳✳✳✳✳✳✳✳✳✳✳✳✳✳✳✳✳✳✳✳✳✳✳✳

Donna Bramhall

Spinster's Emporium/HaberdasherMe

The work of Donna Bramhall, founder of the multifaceted Spinster's Emporium, includes teaching and supporting individuals to explore techniques of textile embellishment. Through HaberdasherMe, she shares her design concepts and the essential sewing skills needed to apply carefully sourced creative trimmings to existing garments.

Donna studied fashion design for eight years, consistently striving to find ways to make her work stand out from that of her peers. Fuelled by the difficulty she encountered when sourcing unique materials, she discovered the breadth and potential of vintage haberdashery, and, having accumulated both knowledge and supplies, she formed Spinster's Emporium.

Donna has a flexible approach to her business, and has explored a variety of outlets for Spinster's, including a shop, studios, creative events and an online presence that endures. HaberdasherMe is her current focus – she has created a retail range for Liberty, and is developing a variety of projects for kits and the press – enabling Donna to respond to her need to travel and take her skills with her.

As a maker, Donna applies a diverse range of materials to her projects, adorning garments with beading, neon colours, metal, wood, stitching, dyeing, print and appliqué. This mix of resources allows her to experiment, producing results that she may not have expected but has achieved through perseverance. She is inspired by culture and costume, and the world is a sourcebook for her to study.

Although she has worked in a variety of settings with a wealth of materials to choose from, Donna now keeps her stash small. Working alone and always carrying a sewing kit, she teaches people how to customize clothes while on the move, stimulated by the sights and materials she encounters.

With haberdashery the focus, Donna Bramhall revives tired garments with inventive stitching, vibrant trimmings and accessories that sparkle.

Constellation Sweater

DONNA BRAMHALL

The HaberdasherMe Constellation Sweater is an attempt to interpret the dazzling stars of the heavens. By using a combination of simple textile techniques, including sewing, beading and bleaching, you can explore the mysteries of the universe from your sofa.

MATERIALS

Old sweatshirt, preferably navy, purple or black, for the space background (fabric content 50% cotton 50% acrylic).

Domestic bleach.

Spray gun.

Paintbrush (optional).

Tailor's chalk.

Sewing machine.

A variety of short, seed and bugle beads.

5mm *(3/16in)*, 8mm *(5/16in)* and 10mm *(3/8in)* cup and star sequins.

Beading needle.

General Knowledge

For inspiration, look at old constellation charts. Leave space around your shapes to give your design impact.

Choose sequins and beads that work with the colour of your sweatshirt. Select metallics and neons for a pop of colour, or opt for bright white to create a sparkling starscape.

Wash the finished sweater delicately by hand and steam press inside out. Excessive direct heat could cause the sequins to disfigure.

1.

Prepare to Bleach

Wear an apron to protect your clothes, and rubber gloves to protect your hands. Place the sweater flat on a clean, dry surface (protect the surface with brown waxed paper if it will react to the bleach). If you are indoors, make sure you are in a well-ventilated room; if you are outdoors, watch out for the direction of the breeze.

The bleach is used to create the back-drop for the glow of the stars. Bleaching the sweater in this way gives added depth to the sequins and beads you will add later on.

2.

Test the Bleach
Apply a small spot of bleach with a paintbrush to the inside of the cuff. Watch what happens: what colour does it turn after three, five or ten minutes, and does the size of the bleached area spread? Time how long it takes to strip the colour from the sweater until you get the desired effect. The effect can vary according to the fabric content, the dye, the thickness of the sweater, and the amount and type of bleach. The longer you leave the bleach on the sweater, the weaker and more damaged the fibres will become. If you leave the bleach on for too long, the fabric can begin to disintegrate.

Mix three parts bleach with one part water in a spray gun. Test the spray gun's spray effect on some paper first, to see how much pressure and distance is needed to create a random starry sky effect. Alternatively, make your own accurate constellations by applying the bleach in spots with a paintbrush.

3.

Bleach the Sweater
Spray the sweater sparingly at first (you can always add more, but it is impossible to remove if you overdo it). Spray the front and the back of the jumper, and don't forget the sleeves. Leave the bleach to take effect for the tested amount of time, before washing it on its own with detergent and softener on a cool cycle. Once it is dry, if necessary repeat the bleaching process until you are happy with the result.

4.

Sew the Constellations
Iron the sweater, then, using tailor's chalk, mark lines joining the bleach spots into constellations. This will act as a guide for your stitches.

Use a large straight stitch (lock stitch) to join the stars together. Because the sweater is a knitted stretchy fabric and the stitch you are using is normally suitable for woven fabrics, it will not be possible to sew a very long continuous straight line, especially at angles, as the fabric can begin to pucker. To avoid this, back-tack and secure the stitches each time you reach a star. Trim all threads on the front and inside of the sweater as you go to avoid tangles.

Iron the sweater on the reverse.

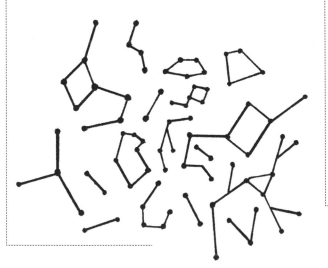

5.

Make Beading Patterns
Apply beads and sequins on top of the star spots. Remember to knot the thread at the bottom each time you sew and pull it through to the right side. Secure with a stitch on the reverse once you have added the beads.

Bead and star

or large cup sequin

Thread star to bead, then back through the star to the reverse of the sweater. Repeat.

Bead and star with bugle, short and seed beads:
For the centre, thread star to bead, then back through the star to the reverse of the sweater. Repeat. Create the surrounding by threading a bugle bead and a short bead together on the same thread. Repeat all the way around the star, and secure the last bead with an extra stitch. Alternatively, attach bugle beads with seed beads in between.

Shooting stars and beads:
Make a row of stars or beads, making sure to secure with at least two stitches each.

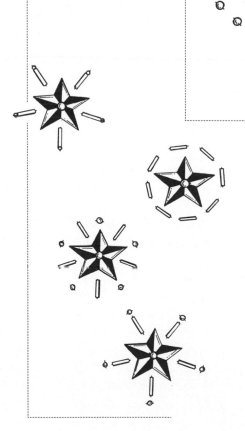

Sophie Strong
Freehand Embroidery Artist

The artist Sophie Strong discovered freehand embroidery by chance. Under the tutelage of Ruth Brompton-Charlesworth at Sumptuosity in York, Sophie was given the chance to replicate illustrations using thread, and took to the skill instantly. Sophie produces wearable art featuring images of individuals and characterful animals. Working with simple lines, she aims to convey the intricacy of her stitching and bring her hand-drawn images to life. Her background is fine art with a focus on sculpture, and she combines a passion for working in three dimensions with an intense style of freehand embroidery.

Sophie's work has a strong focus on powerful human emotions and familial relationships; however, the outcome of this interest is not one specific image or product. Responding to what is happening in the present, whether in her own life or current affairs, Sophie's embroidery is evocative, using thread to give texture and detail, and to provoke a response.

She works from home, with her inspiration and sewn projects hanging on the walls and easels of her shared living space. She keeps only a large sewing toolbox and a small collection of fabric, preferring to seek out the right material to fit the aesthetic of each piece. To allow the stitches to speak, she works with plain, hardwearing fabrics in muted tones, applying colour with thread.

For Sophie, creating is an intense and serious process. Generally sketching from photographs, she draws an image in pencil on paper, traces it and then commits it to cloth, painstakingly sewing through the paper and then using tweezers to remove the fragments between the threads. Sophie's conviction that drawing directly on the fabric inhibits her creativity means that the act of making a piece is, for her, a real time commitment.

Sophie Strong stitches reality, documenting images in thread to make wearable work and art pieces that are evocative, beautiful and provoking.

Cameo Brooch

SOPHIE
STRONG

Cutting portraits, generally in profile, from black card became popular in the mid-eighteenth century. This project makes an ideal keepsake for a special occasion. As with a modern-day locket, you could create a lasting image of a special person or even a whole set to represent your nearest and dearest. Choose pastel tones of leather and muted tones for the linen. For threads, try neon colours for more impact. Select a dark colour for the portrait outline.

MATERIALS

A4 sheet of white paper.

Masking tape.

Torch or Anglepoise-style lamp.

Scanner, computer and printer.

Tracing paper.

Piece of linen, approx. 15cm (5⅞in) square.

Embroidery hoop (optional).

Sewing machine with lowerable feed dogs.

Darning/free-motion embroidery foot.

Machine embroidery thread.

2 pieces leather in the same or contrasting colours, each approx. 15cm (5⅞in) square.

Ballpoint pen.

Brooch pin.

Fabric glue.

Leather hand-sewing needle (optional).

1.

Capture a Portrait: The Traditional Method

Tape the paper to a wall and shine the light at it. Sit sideways between the light and the wall so that your profile appears on the paper, and ask a willing volunteer to trace your silhouette. Remove the paper from the wall and tidy up any uneven lines. Scan the image into the computer, resize it to 5 x 6cm *(2 x 2⅜in)* and print. Attach the tracing paper to the image with tape and trace a single neat line around it. To allow a practice run, create two identical traced images from the drawing.

You could, of course, trace from an existing photograph instead.

2.

Embroider the Cameo
Attach the tracing-paper drawing to the linen with masking tape, making sure no tape touches the area to be sewn. If you wish, for extra stability, put the fabric into an embroidery hoop with the larger ring underneath.

Place the fabric in the sewing machine. Lower the embroidery foot so the needle is on the line of your drawing. Moving the linen slowly, trace the line of your silhouette carefully with short, straight stitches.

Remember to reverse on to the line when you have completed the embroidery, to secure your stitches. If your silhouette includes a neckline, you could create a necklace effect by embroidering a line across the neck using thread in a complementary colour. When you have completed your sewing, remove the fabric from the sewing machine and cut any loose threads.

Remove the embroidery hoop and masking tape, and carefully peel off the tracing paper to reveal the image.

3.

Attach the Linen to the Leather
Place the embroidery on top of the leather, but do not pin at this stage as you may mark the fabrics. Put both layers into the embroidery hoop.

Use thread in a different colour to machine stitch a rough outline around the portrait, 2mm *(³⁄₃₂in)* away from the original line. Do not sew over the silhouette outline. Remember to change the bobbin thread as well as the top thread.

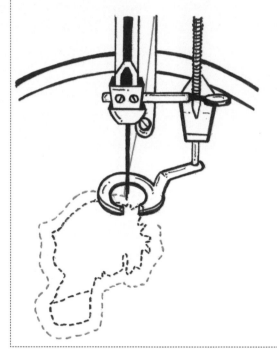

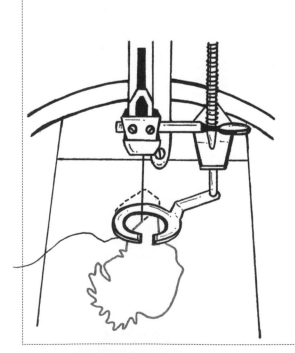

4.

Frame the Cameo

Trim away the linen 2mm *(³⁄₃₂in)* from the stitched line, without cutting through the leather.

Embroider over the outer line using short horizontal stitches, until the linen edge is no longer visible. Remember to move the fabric slowly to control the stitching.

To add further detail, repeat the process with thread in another colour, this time making the lines less dense.

Cut an oval around your line of embroidery, leaving a 5mm *(³⁄₁₆in)* gap around the edge.

Repeat the sewing process one last time, sewing over the edge of the leather to give the cameo a bold border.

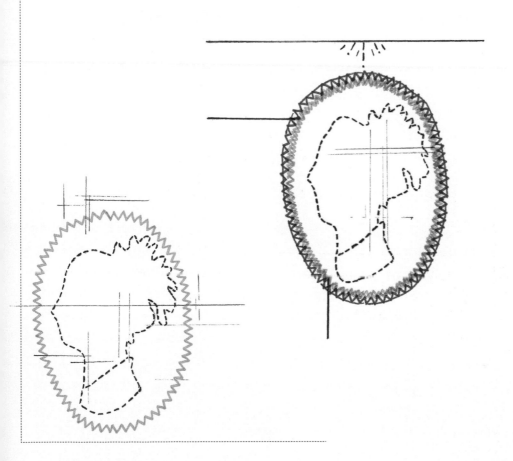

5.

Add the Inscription
Using a ballpoint pen, write an inscription on the backing leather, leaving a space to attach a brooch pin. Slowly sew over the pen marks using short, straight stitches.

Cut the backing piece of leather to the same size and shape as the front. Sew the brooch pin to the back, covering your stitches with a small scrap of leather or fabric of your choice.

6.

Assemble the Brooch
Apply a thin layer of fabric glue to the wrong side of each piece of leather, press together and leave to dry.

When the glue has dried, hand or machine sew over the raw edges using the same thread as the border.

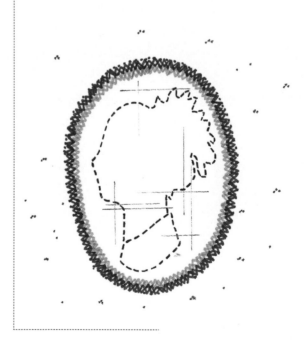

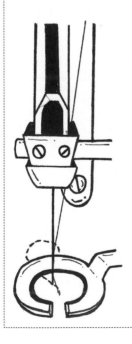

General Knowledge
Use the appropriate machine needle for the type of fabric you choose.

The switch to lower the feed dogs on a sewing machine is found at the back of machines with top-loading bobbins, or revealed by moving the free arm on machines with front-loading bobbins.

You will find the material easier to manoeuvre if you use a larger piece than you need. Cut it to size later.

Kim Davis

Oh, Sweet Joy

Kim Davis designs vibrantly colourful, on-trend and accessible sewing projects and products with wide appeal. Her work is aimed at those who want to create something individual, with a limited range of materials in a short time frame. The focus, however, is not on making something rushed, but enjoying the process and the resulting individual piece, usually an accessory.

Pattern and colour are fundamental in Kim's projects. She opts for bold solid colours, stripes, dots and small florals, all selected to enhance the wardrobe of the wearer. She revels in the search for bright fabrics that will enhance her ideas, browsing local fabric stores, researching trends and taking time to form a cohesive collection. Recognizing the role fabric designers play in her work, she holds the textile designs of Anna Maria Horner and Leah Duncan in high esteem, and promotes other artists and designer-makers through her blog.

In her own products and tutorials, Kim advocates a passion for everyday creativity. Social media enables her to connect with other makers and share with her readers, enriching their experience of the crafting world as well as her own. With this focus on sharing, she extends the traditional notion of learning at home to a wider world: while sewing with a relative might still be how young people learn, for adults, learning online can be the only way to gain new experience and techniques.

Working from a shared spare room, Kim functions amid the demands of family life. She works best in some mess, surrounding herself with projects in progress. The enthusiasm that resonates through her work encourages others to make for pleasure.

Practical meets fun in Kim Davis's world of colourful sewn accessories, created with the essential tools of the trade in her organized craft space.

Paper-Bag Skirt

KIM
DAVIS

Sewists often have enviable fabric stashes. With just under 1m *(39in)* of fabric, you can create a simple garment very quickly. Using this skirt as a base, you can play with different fabrics, trims and shapes to make the ideal skirt for your style.

MATERIALS

1m *(39in)* fabric.
Tape measure.
2.5cm *(1in)* wide elastic.
Dressmaking pins.
Sewing machine.
Large safety pin.

1.

Prepare Fabric and Elastic
Measure yourself before cutting two identical pieces of fabric. For the width, measure the widest part of your hips and divide that measurement by two. Then add 7.5cm *(3in)* for seam allowance and to add more of a paper-bag effect.

For the length, place one end of the tape measure where you would like the skirt to sit on your waist, and proceed to where you would like it to hit on your leg. Add 10cm *(4in)* to that measurement for the bottom hem and the top paper-bag element.

To prepare the elastic, subtract 5cm *(2in)* from your waist measurement, measure out elastic to the same length and cut.

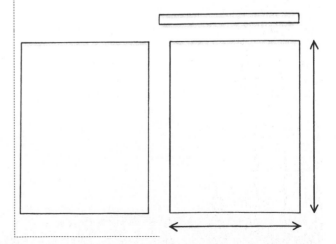

2.

Pin and Sew
Sides and Hem

Line up the fabric pieces with right sides facing, and pin along the side seams. Sew along the sides leaving a 1cm *(⅜in)* seam allowance, then finish the raw edges.

Fold up the bottom hem 1cm *(⅜in)* and press all the way around. Fold up another 1cm *(⅜in)* so that the raw edge is inside the finished edge and not exposed. Stitch all the way around the hem, starting at a side seam.

3.

Pin and Sew
Paper-Bag Waist

With the skirt still wrong side out, fold the top down 6cm *(2⅜in)*, press and pin in place. Stitch along the edge of the fabric, leaving an opening 2.5cm *(1in)* wide on a side seam for the elastic.

To make the casing for the elastic, sew just over 2.5cm *(1in)* above the line you just sewed, without leaving a gap.

Pin one end of the elastic to the top of the skirt to secure. Use a large safety pin to pull the elastic through the casing, a little at a time.

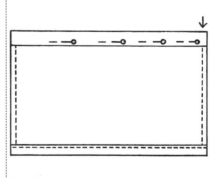

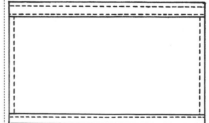

4.

Finish

Once the elastic is all the way through, pin the ends together and try the skirt on. Trim the elastic as needed. When you have the desired fit, overlap the edges and zigzag stitch back and forth to secure. Sew up the gap in the waistband.

General Knowledge

There are a variety of methods for finishing seams. For this project, use a zigzag stitch, trim with pinking shears or use an overlocker if you have one.

The waist and hip measurements are important. To avoid the skirt being too baggy, take measurements in your underwear. The skirt should sit high on the waist to create the most flattering silhouette, and so that it can be worn with a fitted top tucked in.

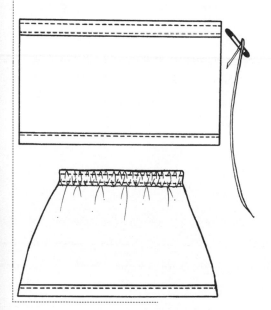

Sarah Burford

Curious Pip

Sarah Burford's illustrations and handmade art dolls reflect her lifelong passion for theatre, cinema and art. Each doll is reminiscent of another time, a character from a past where glamour reigned.

Formerly an actor, Sarah was always attracted to costumes and took pleasure in the transformation clothing, wigs and make-up afforded her. As a child, she watched old films, including the choreography of Busby Berkeley; this education inspired her to draw, replicating the on-screen outfits in her own illustrations.

Sarah draws every day, and paints using gouache, watercolour and acrylic. Her workspace includes open shelves displaying the tools of her art. Her dolls are predominantly hand-sewn, with visible stitching that forms part of the costume. Sarah does not strive for perfection; the fabric is sculpted in twists, ties and folds to achieve a nostalgic style of dress. The life of each doll is fully imagined, and Sarah's fabric stash forms a dressing-up box of possible outfits. Her dolls are made with the intention that they should be permanent, and with time will age and decay in a beautiful manner.

The pace of Sarah's work is unhurried, with plenty of time devoted to each piece. This approach avoids the frenetic style of production that can trouble her peers. Of other makers, Sarah is attracted to the imagination of Mister Finch and the cornucopia of handmade items produced by Jess Quinn.

Being fascinated by the past, Sarah collects pre-loved dolls as part of her research; she is attracted to the everyday accoutrements of life both in her home and in her style of dress. There is a clear confidence in her style, an instinct that enables her to trust her own taste and convey it in her portfolio.

Among her collection of inspirational artworks and well-loved toys, Sarah Burford's illustrations and art dolls are evocative of past glamour and style.

Circus Wall Decoration

SARAH BURFORD

This wall hanging was inspired by Sarah's love of old circus troupes and the choreography of Busby Berkeley. Each character is created from a set of basic templates; add your own embellishments to bring each performer to life. When choosing a fabric for the main body, select a cotton or calico that can be tea-dyed to achieve different skin tones. The finished size of the wall hanging is 38cm *(15in)* in diameter.

1.

Create a Body Base
Cut out two body shapes from the calico and carefully stitch the head section together using a 5mm *(³⁄₁₆in)* seam allowance.

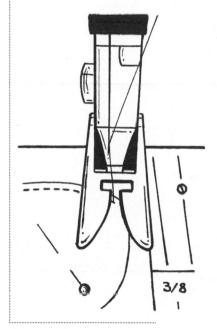

MATERIALS

Character templates from CD.

Calico, 30cm *(12in)* square for each character.

Sewing machine.

Polyester stuffing.

Merino wool in various colours.

Needle and thread.

Felt in various colours.

Fabric pens.

Sequins.

Acrylic paint.

Craft varnish.

Pompoms.

Fabric glue.

Ribbon.

Fine paintbrush.

6 small polystyrene balls.

Craft wire.

Newspaper.

PVA glue.

Fringing and gold wavy trim.

Fabric scraps.

Masking tape.

1 empty cotton reel.

Small piece of thick card.

Black cotton thread.

30cm *(12in)*, 20cm *(7⁷⁄₈in)* and 10cm *(4in)* embroidery hoops.

Additional embellishments of your choice.

2.

Add Arms

Cut out two arm shapes from the calico, stitch, turn inside out and stuff. With the body shape laid flat, lift up the top piece and sandwich the arms between the body pieces. Sew around the edges, leaving a gap to flip the character right side out, and stuff well.

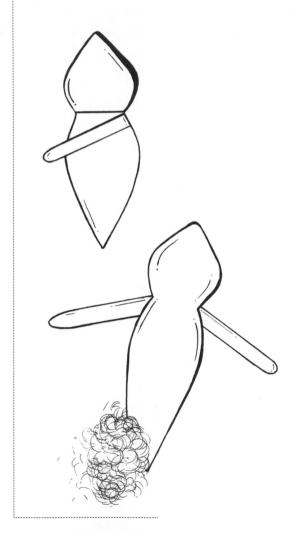

3.

Create Characters:
The Sideshow Mermaid

To make the mermaid's hair, create curls in white merino wool and stitch to the head. Felt it to add extra definition. Create a head garland by sewing on flowers or embellishments of your choice.

Cut out a red felt cape using the template, blanket stitch the edges and sew on fabric stars. For a shabby look, cut the stars with raw edges.

Draw a face on with fabric pen, gently iron to prevent it from running, then stitch over the top of each detail with a doubled sewing thread.

For the tail, cut two identical tail shapes from felt using the template. Sew them together by hand or machine with a 5mm *(3/16in)* seam allowance, then turn right sides out and stuff the bottom. Embellish one side with sequins to make glamorous scales. Make the fan part of the tail by cutting two identical felt shapes. Blanket stitch them together, leaving an opening at the top, and sew on to the bottom of the tail. Stitch the whole tail to the body of the mermaid.

The Clown

Give your clown a patterned costume with red acrylic paint and varnish. Add pompoms to his tummy using fabric glue. Make clown shoes by cutting out two identical shapes in black felt and blanket stitching around the bottom and sides, leaving a gap at the top to sew them on to his body. Tie a scrap of ribbon around his neck in a bow. Using the template, cut two felt pieces for the hat, blanket stitch together and attach to the top of his head. Use fabric pens or paint and a fine brush to create the face.

Make the juggling balls by threading six polystyrene balls on to a length of craft wire long enough to reach between the clown's arms, and loop around the wrists. Cover the balls with a thin layer of papier mâché, then paint and varnish.

The Showgirl

Dress your showgirl by stitching individual sequins on to the torso to make the top of her romper. Add a skirt by stitching on a length of fringing. Get creative with beads and trimmings to make bangles, earrings, a necklace and a feather headdress, and sew on gold wavy trim to create her hair. Use fabric pens or paint and a fine brush to create a glamorous expression, and sew over the parts you want to accentuate.

The Tattooed Lady

Use sparkly netting for her ruffle, and sequins and various bits of haberdashery for her headdress. Draw the tattoos with a fabric pen, iron to set them and colour with acrylic paint. To make her hair, create curls in black merino wool and stitch to the head; felt it to add extra definition. Use fabric pens or paint and a fine brush to create her face, sewing some parts for emphasis.

The Ringmaster

Paint on a typical ringmaster outfit using acrylic paint, then varnish. Embellish his costume with gold trim. To create the ringmaster's boots, use the template to cut two identical felt pieces. Blanket stitch them together, leaving the top open, and stitch to the body.

To make his hat, use masking tape to attach an empty cotton reel to a circular piece of thick card. Apply a few layers of papier mâché, leave to dry, paint then varnish. Sew the hat to the ringmaster's head and use a little black merino wool for hair. Use fabric pens or paint and a fine brush to create the face, sewing over the features you want to accentuate.

The Strongman

Paint on trousers with acrylic paint and varnish, add a tattoo with fabric pen and give your strongman some rather thin strands of hair with black cotton. Use fabric pens or paint and a fine brush to create the face, sew for emphasis and finish with a spectacular moustache.

4.

Make the Framework

Make the framework from the inner parts of the embroidery hoops. Paint them bright red and varnish. Join the framework with short lengths of craft wire and hang using a long red ribbon.

Arrange the characters in a circle and stitch their hands together. Sew a ribbon to the back of each head and tie to the outer part of the framework.

General Knowledge
When stuffing the characters, work with small pieces of stuffing and push down to the furthest point using a knitting needle.

To tea dye, immerse the fabric in stewed tea, covering the container to prevent the fabric from floating up. Check it regularly for your desired colour. Hang up to dry.

To make papier mâché, tear up small pieces of newspaper and soak in a paste of three parts glue and one part water. Apply to your chosen surface.

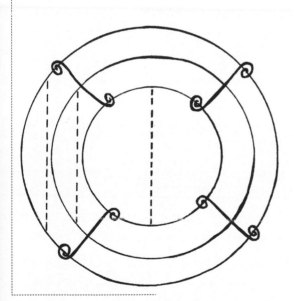

Rachelle Francis

Embroidery Designer

Rachelle Francis is an embroidery designer, creating one-off, directional embroidery, embellishment and garment details for the couture and designer fashion markets. Her focus is on craftsmanship, often intricate and experimental, challenging traditional notions of what embroidery is. Rachelle really understands her materials and how to handle and apply them, and it is this deep knowledge that enables her to play confidently with colour and scale.

Rachelle focuses on innovation, breaking the conventions of recognized techniques such as smocking and appliqué to make something unique and challenge the expectations of her audience. Well versed in the industry, and with a particular admiration of Christopher Kane's use of embellishment, she works instinctively, seeking out fabrics and trims to suit her purpose and fuel her imagination. She constantly adds to her portfolio, reinventing beads and sequins into new building blocks for couture fabrics.

As a child, Rachelle was encouraged to draw and was heavily influenced by a collection of creative patterns produced by her mother during the 1970s. This approach to making with abandon enabled Rachelle to feel free to generate her own designs, using materials to make something out of nothing and then home in on the smaller elements, focusing on perfecting every tiny detail.

It is this attention to detail and experimentation that are evident in Rachelle's textiles, showing the application of originality in a controlled form while creating for a purpose. Working behind the scenes of the fashion industry, Rachelle sells her work and, with it, the copyright to her designs. Ultimately, she would like to achieve recognition through the production of her own small collection of hand-embellished garments, under her own name.

Rachelle Francis's tactile inspirations hang about her workspace, including a treasured felt-tip illustration by her mother, Diana Francis.

Chic Covered Buttons

RACHELLE
FRANCIS

You can mix and match from the following button techniques to build a wide range of designs. Play with scale, colour and technique to create your own collection of chic buttons. Apply them on their own, or in clusters and patterns to embellish a neckline, make a one-off brooch, a cuff or a jewel for a purse.

1.

Cover the Buttons
Draw around a circle template on to fabric and cut out. Use the template that comes with the self-cover buttons, or make your own. Sew a running stitch close to the edge of the circle, leaving the threads long and hanging at each side. Place the button head face down on the reverse of the fabric circle and pull the threads up to gather the fabric tightly around the stem of the button. Secure the fabric in place with the button back.

MATERIALS

Self-cover buttons in a variety of sizes.
Small pieces of fabric.
Needle and invisible thread.
Large, flat round sequins.
Tulle.
A variety of beads, including giant bugle beads.

General Knowledge
Invisible thread is prone to tangling, so work in short lengths to avoid this. When you have finished sewing, apply a short piece of tape to the end to avoid it unravelling in storage.

2.

Cover the Sequins with Tulle

Cut a circle of tulle at least 1cm *(³/₈in)* wider all around than the sequin. Using a similar method to covering buttons, sew a running stitch close to the edge of the circle, leaving the threads long and hanging at each side. Place the sequin head on the tulle and pull the threads up to gather the fabric tightly around the sequin. Tie a few knots to secure.

3.

Make the Centrepiece Petals

Cover a 38mm *(1¹/₂in)* self-cover button with fabric, then cover five sequins with a layer of tulle. Thread a needle and tie a knot in the end of the thread. Pull the needle through the top centre of the covered button. Stitch each sequin on around the button shape, stitching through the holes in the tulle and layering the sequins as you go.

Secure the sequins at the outer edge of the button with extra stitches if needed.

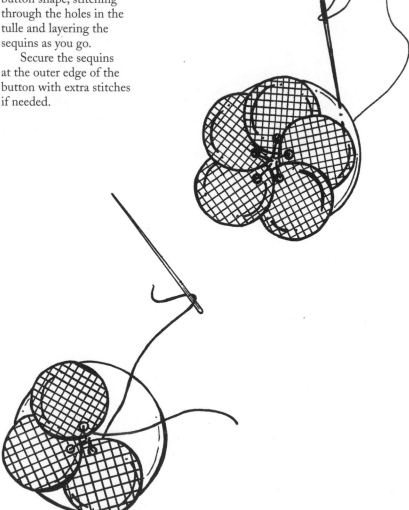

4.

Add Legs and Finish the Centrepiece

To make the legs, secure the thread on the bottom outer edge of the button, thread the needle with a giant bugle bead followed by a small bead, and pull the thread through. Return the needle around the side of the small bead, then back up through the hole in the bottom of the bugle bead, pulling through to the top. Knot next to the original knot on the outer edge of the button. Repeat for the remaining two legs.

Make a smaller version of the button with legs by covering a 10mm (³⁄₈in) self-cover button with fabric.

Create three shorter legs and stitch them to the top of the small button. Then sew the smaller button in the centre of the tulle-covered sequins.

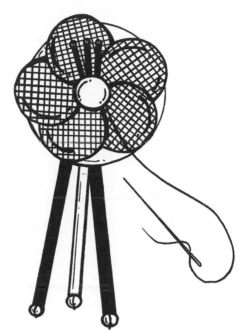

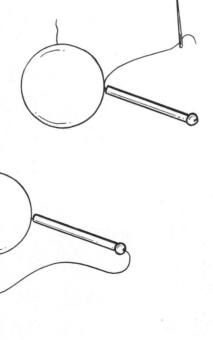

5.

Idea: Sequin with Beaded Halo

Cover a 19mm *(³/₄in)* or 29mm *(1¹/₈in)* self-cover button with fabric, then cover one sequin with a layer of tulle. Using invisible thread, stitch a row of beads around the outer edge of the sequin, passing the needle through the holes in the tulle. Secure the sequin to the button by stitching through the tulle on the left and right edges of the sequin.

6.

Idea: Dotty Button

Cover a 19mm *(³/₄in)* or 29mm *(1¹/₈in)* self-cover button with fabric. Stitch a random pattern of beads all over the button, including around the outer edges.

7.

Idea: Sequin Fan

Cover a 19mm *(³/₄in)* or 29mm *(1¹/₈in)* self-cover button with fabric, then cover four sequins with a layer of tulle. Fold all the sequins in half with the top hole in the centre.

Secure the thread on top of the button, close to one edge, then thread the needle through the outer edge of the sequin and secure the edge of the sequin to the button. Pass the needle through to the centre of the button, then thread the needle through the centre fold of the remaining sequins, one by one.

Sew the outer edge of the last sequin to the outer edge of the button, and fan the sequins out into position. Secure the tops and bottoms of each sequin into the fan position, each time passing the needle through the tulle and button fabric.

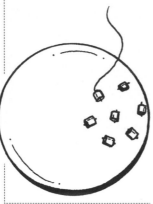

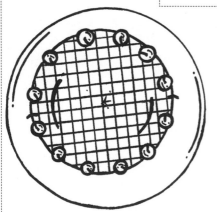

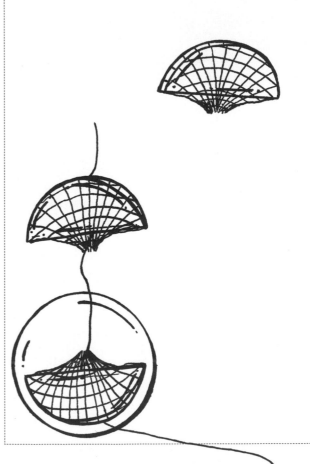

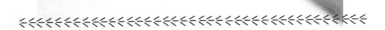

Megan Hunt

Project Designer

Megan Hunt has a wealth of experience in the design world, and her work is constantly evolving. She creates wedding and party dresses, adapts her original embroidered felt flower brooches to thrill brides with everlasting bouquets, and, most lately, champions emerging independent designers with her online fashion store Hello Holiday.

Operating from a studio apartment on a busy street in Omaha, Nebraska, Megan takes in the bustle below as she works. The domesticity of this set-up, including the presence of her young daughter, echoes the way Megan first experienced textiles. Learning from her mother, a quilter, Megan was surrounded by stacks of fabric available for experimentation. She recalls the pleasure of pulling threaded needles from her mother's pincushion and sewing running stitches through the scraps. This pleasure in sewing and the notion of being connected to other makers has never left her.

Megan's approach to her creative work is exceptionally social. Her blog, Princess Lasertron, gives her audience the opportunity to connect with her work. She values the notion of there being a face behind a brand and recognizes the importance of developing a relationship with her patrons. Although she operates through the online world, she keeps a very clear sense that everything is real, and her interaction with her customers is testament to that ethos.

Megan takes inspiration from her local community of creative entrepreneurs and their ambitious work ethic, and seeks to support them in return. She adopts the same approach when sourcing materials, and recommends taking the time to seek out and work with what is available locally. Megan unites the real and the virtual with aplomb, connecting the joy of creating in both spheres.

With a wealth of materials, Megan Hunt's space is packed with sewing paraphernalia, providing creative stimulus for both herself and her young daughter.

Pleated Headband

MEGAN HUNT

This headband in versatile felt, with a style reminiscent of the 1920s, is a short project, ideal for a weekend afternoon. Manipulating the felt using folds can be a challenge, requiring confident handling. However, felt is forgiving and allows the sewist to test shapes and pin with the knowledge that any pin marks or light folds can be hidden in the fibres.

1.

Secure the Elastic
Join the two felt pieces by the short edges with a 2.5cm *(1in)* seam, then trim to make a piece 115cm *(45¼in)* long.

Create a simple box pleat at one end of the felt strip. Begin by marking every 2.5cm *(1in)* along the length of the felt. Fold one end of the felt strip up 5cm *(2in)* and down 2.5cm *(1in)* to make a Z-shaped pleat. Sandwich the end of the elastic between the two pleated felt layers and stitch to secure.

MATERIALS

2 pieces of felt, each 60 x 5cm *(23⅝ x 2in)*.

Sewing machine.

Marking pencil, pen or chalk.

15cm *(5⅞in)* black ribbed elastic.

Paper.

Square of felt, 25 x 25cm *(9⅞ x 9⅞in)*.

Button, 2.5cm *(1in)* diameter.

Embroidery thread.

General Knowledge
To work a needle through layers of felt, wiggle rather than pull.

When sewing the elastic, match the line of the machine stitching on either side for a symmetrical look.

2.

Make the Pleats

Use the marks as a guideline to fold the felt every 5cm *(2in)* along the strip, bringing the folded edges together on the wrong side. Pin to secure the pleats, leaving an extra 5cm *(2in)* at the end to attach the other side of the elastic.

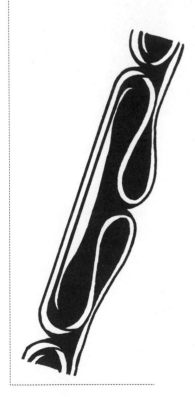

3.

Sew the Pleats

Machine sew two lines of running stitch, one on either side of the centre of the strip, to secure the pleats.

Test the fit of the headband, adjusting the length of the elastic accordingly. Fold the other side of the felt up 5cm *(2in)* and down 2.5cm *(1in)* to make another Z-pleat. Slide the other end of the elastic into the pleat and stitch to secure.

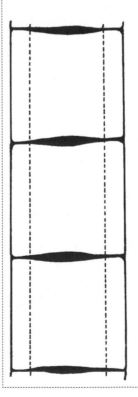

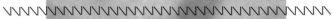

4.

Create the Flower

Draw a simple petal shape on paper and cut out to make a template. Use it to cut 25 petals from the remaining felt.

Cut a circle of felt 4cm *(1⅝in)* in diameter and sew the petals on one by one, starting from the outside and working in. Add a button to the centre of the flower. Sew the flower to the headband.

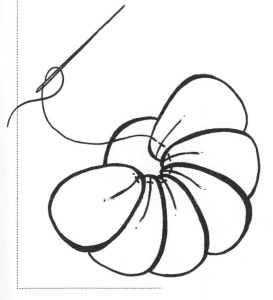

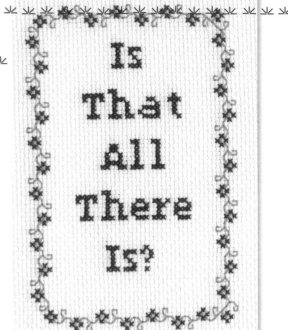

Is That All There Is?

It's Not Mean If It's Hilarious

subversive cross stitch®

Julie Jackson

Subversive Cross Stitch

The founder of Subversive Cross Stitch, Julie Jackson, shares her cross-stitch patterns, tips and supplies with the world from her home office in Texas. First attracted to cross stitch by its sheer simplicity, Julie enjoys the challenge of the design process – operating within the limitations of the gridded cloth to create workable and attractive pieces. The contrast between the monotonous history of stitched samplers and Julie's rule-breaking approach is clear as she creates a controlled chaos designed to be sewn in tiny traditional crosses.

Julie has always been artistic, but she came into her own when she started making her own pieces. Subversive Cross Stitch grew out of her frustration at work more than a decade ago. Seeking an outlet for her rage, Julie stitched a sampler with a four-letter word, and in that moment discovered a new career.

As a self-proclaimed internet junkie, Julie increased her business through online sharing, as part of the do-it-yourself movement. Her intention was to encourage others to stitch funny or forbidden things for themselves and to take pleasure in the process. She enjoys the camaraderie that can be found in the virtual world, and the possibility for everyone to share and find a community. Although her slogans can be amusingly insulting, Julie's outlook is magnanimous, promoting a mutually supportive society.

She is constantly busy, and there is little scope for personal projects or social sewing; during leisure time she adds to a collection of reworked vintage stitched pieces, ripping out the old words and replacing them with her own. This artistic outlet is kept for herself despite requests to exhibit in galleries, and it is through this that she can experience the same pleasure her cross-stitch community feels.

Julie Jackson's patterns and stitched images prove the cathartic nature of hand sewing, telling it how it is in Aida and thread.

This is Where the Magic Happens Cross Stitch

JULIE
JACKSON

Cross stitch, one of the oldest forms of embroidery, is used to create decorative stitched pieces and embellish clothes and accessories. This cross stitch does not need to be perfect; the emphasis is on enjoying the process and the result, having written an unexpected phrase in thread.

MATERIALS

 Cross-stitch pattern from CD.

14 count Aida, 17.5 x 23cm *(7 x 9in)*.

Embroidery hoop (optional).

Cross-stitch thread.

Needle.

Stitchery Tape or cardboard.

Sewing thread.

1.

To Begin

Find the approximate centre of the pattern, then find the approximate centre of the fabric. You will begin stitching one of the elements near the centre of the pattern. Working this way, from the centre out, will ensure that you avoid stitching off the edge of the material. Place the fabric in an embroidery hoop if you like.

To begin stitching, bring the threaded needle up from the back of the fabric, leaving a tail of thread about 2.5cm *(1in)* behind the fabric. Stitch the next five or six stitches over the tail, then clip off the extra thread. To end, weave the needle back through the last five or six stitches and clip the thread short.

2.

To Cross Stitch

There are two methods. The first is to work a row of half-stitches, then work back to complete the Xs. Use this method for most stitching. The second method is to complete each X as you go. Use this for vertical rows of stitches.

The main thing is that each X crosses in the same direction; that is, the top thread of the X should always slant in the same direction. It doesn't matter which way they slant, but if they are mixed, the finished piece will look uneven. Relax as you stitch. Your stitches should lie flat on the fabric and not distort the holes or the fabric.

3.

To Change Colour

Sometimes a colour will be needed for only a few stitches before jumping to another area. Most of the time you should end off and start again, but if the distance is short you can carry the thread along the back. Be aware that the thread might show through white fabric.

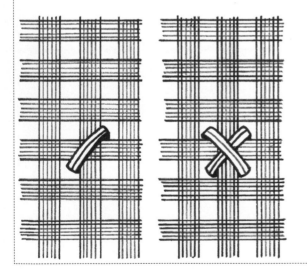

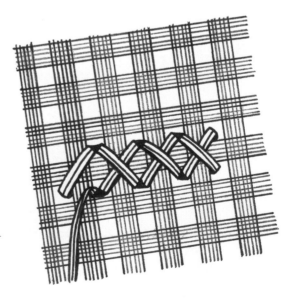

4.

To Finish

Hand wash the finished piece in cold water with a gentle or very dilute detergent. Let it dry naturally, then press with an iron.

To mount your work, use Stitchery Tape or a hard cardboard insert. Centre the finished piece on the cardboard and sew in big zigzags on the back so that the fabric is taut on the front. Be sure it is taut both horizontally and vertically.

General Knowledge

Thread:
The most common cross-stitch floss has six strands bundled together in what seems like one piece. For this project, you will use only two of those strands at a time.

Embroidery hoop:
You will probably need an embroidery hoop to hold the fabric taut while you stitch, especially if you're a beginner. It doesn't matter what material the hoop is made of; just make sure it clamps the material all the way around.

Jaime Jennings and Amber Corcoran
Fancy Tiger Crafts

Jaime Jennings and Amber Corcoran form the Fancy Tiger Crafts emporium in Denver, Colorado. The pairing developed through a long-standing friendship and a mutual passion for yarn and textiles.

Both Jaime and Amber were raised in creative homes, with mothers who passed on their expertise. They grew up with the notion that they could knit or sew anything, a no-fear approach to craft that stood them in good stead. First learning to knit, they continued to develop, then through opening Fancy Tiger their capability grew in line with the varied materials and excellent craft tutors they employ.

Jaime is predominantly a garment maker, and has developed a wardrobe of handmade clothes. With a wealth of supplies at hand, she works on one project at a time, sourcing the right pattern for the task and challenging herself to try new techniques.

Amber's aim, meanwhile, is to sample every craft. Like Jaime, she creates her own clothing and is inspired by the community of makers that frequent Fancy Tiger. She designs her own patterns, driven by colour and texture. She is an impatient maker, keen to complete each piece in order to move on to the next. She takes full advantage of the talent displayed at Fancy Tiger, relishing the opportunity to learn the sewing tricks of those around her.

Jaime and Amber use their blog to communicate with a wider audience, sharing their projects, showcasing designers and displaying what can be made with their wares. The value of learning is a focus at Fancy Tiger. With a workspace dedicated to craft classes and a wealth of teaching experience within their team, Jaime and Amber are passing on the skills and confidence imparted in childhood.

Fancy Tiger Crafts, a creative collaboration born out of a love of handmade. Jaime and Amber share a wealth of craft supplies in their Denver store.

Patchwork Coasters

AMBER CORCORAN

Working with patchwork on a small scale is a great way to try out this time-honoured process, and will also help you to understand how colour and pattern work together. Using scraps gives the sewist the opportunity to revisit fabrics stashed away and create a product that is both useful and beautiful. For this project, use a 6mm *(¼in)* seam allowance for all piecing.

MATERIALS

Fabric scraps: you can use pieces as small as 5cm *(2in)* square for these little patchworks, but you will want a few that are at least 12.5cm *(5in)* square for the backs.

Sewing machine.

Cotton wadding, 30.5cm *(12in)* square.

QUARTER CABIN

1.
Cut Out
Cut a mix of light and dark scraps into one 5cm *(2in)* square and four 3 x 25cm *(1⅛ x 9⅞in)* strips.

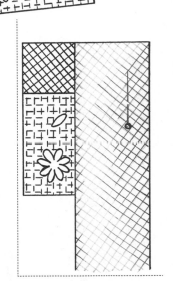

2.
Piece
Starting with the square piece and one strip, put right sides together and line the strip up with the top of the square and one end of the strip with the left-hand side of the square. Seam together and cut off the excess length of the strip. Seam the rest of the strip along the right-hand side of the square. Cut any excess off.

Now, using the patched piece and another strip, put right sides together, line the strip up with the top of the patched piece and one end of the strip with a side of the patched piece. Seam together. Cut off the excess length of the strip. Using the rest of the strip, seam it along the right-hand side of the patched piece. Cut any excess off. Repeat twice more for a total of four rows of strips around the square. Now try the next technique or skip ahead to the finishing instructions.

Above right in picture, Quarter Cabin; below, Wonky Star.

WONKY STAR

1.

Cut Out

Cut scraps of dark fabric into eight 5cm *(2in)* square pieces. Use different prints for a patchwork look, or matching fabric.

Cut light scraps into one 5cm *(2in)* square piece and four 7cm *(2³/4in)* square pieces; these will make up the star.

Set the smaller light square aside and stack the other four together. Cut them in half on the diagonal to make eight right-angle triangles.

2.

Piece the First Triangle

Start with one dark square and one light triangle. Place them right sides together with the triangle on top, and the right angle of the triangle just a little inside the corner of the square. You can make slight adjustments to the angle for more wonkiness, but make sure that once the seam is sewn the triangle, when pressed over, will cover the corner of the square. Sew a seam 6mm *(1/4in)* from the long edge of the triangle. Repeat with three more dark squares and three more light triangles. Press the seams so that the right sides of the triangles show.

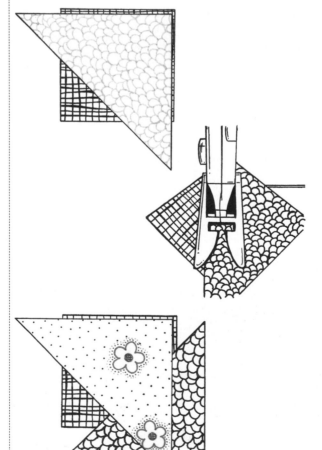

3.

Piece the Second Triangle

Now, take one patchworked square and another light triangle. Place them right sides together with the triangle on top. The right-angle corner of the triangle should be nearest a corner of the square that has the previous seam on it, and the right angle of the triangle just a little inside the corner of the square. You can make slight adjustments to the angle for more wonkiness, but make sure that once the seam is sewn the triangle, when pressed over, will cover the corner of the square. Sew a seam 6mm *(1/4in)* from the long edge of the triangle. Repeat with three more patchworked squares and three more triangles. Press the seams so that the right sides of the triangles show. You should now have two star points on four squares. Cut down the excess triangle fabric so the piece measures 5cm *(2in)* square again.

4.

Lay Out Pieces

Lay out the pieces as follows:

1st row:
Dark square, star points up, dark square.

2nd row:
Star points left, light square, star points right.

3rd row:
Dark square, star points down, dark square.

Join the pieces for each row separately and press. Seam the three rows together and press.

5.

Finish the Coasters

For each coaster, cut a piece of fabric and a piece of wadding to the same size as the coaster. Place the front and back of the coaster right sides together. Lay the wadding on the wrong side of the coaster back. Seam all three layers together around all four corners and three sides, leaving most of one side open for turning. Turn right side out and press flat, taking care to press the seam allowance of 6mm *(¼in)* in along the open side. Top stitch around the edge of the coaster to close.

General Knowledge

Patchwork and quilting commonly go hand in hand. You can also add quilting to your coaster by stitching 3mm *(⅛in)* outside and around the wonky star, or around the inside of a few of the strips.

The choice of fabric is important. Quilting-weight cotton is ideal, but if you are using scraps from your fabric stash, make sure they all wash the same way, otherwise some may shrink and distort the coasters.

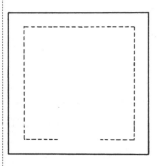

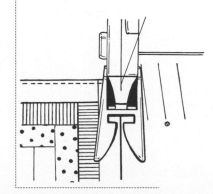

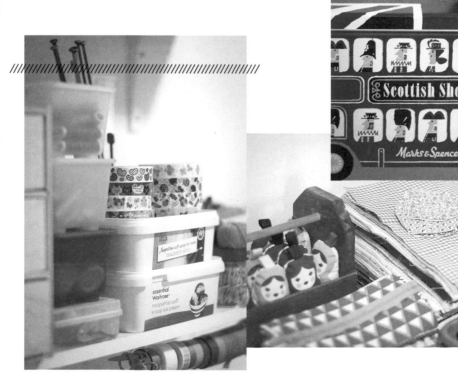

Andrea Tong-Tucker

Roxypop

Andrea Tong-Tucker is connected to a variety of branches of the handmade world. She accesses the creative community through social media, event management and working with skilled local designer-makers, as well as by producing her own range of products.

Andrea's creative outlet, Roxypop, specializes in sewn and crocheted fabric goods with a practical purpose. Andrea acquires fabric from a variety of sources, including estate sales. She has a particular affection for discontinued gingham in unusual colours, and consistently uses it to line her zipped purses and gadget cases, making them distinctively hers.

Having sampled a variety of crafts as a child, Andrea learned to sew and crochet as an adult and eventually gained the confidence to design her own patterns and make a range of accessories. At first selling through craft fairs, she now makes her Roxypop products available through retailers across Canada.

Andrea's experience of outdated craft events led to the creation of Got Craft? in 2007, a biannual handmade event she curated with her husband, Robert. Intended to offer the craft community a different marketplace from the more traditional craft fair, it enjoyed great success. Andrea and Robert's aim to bring together a community that fosters handmade and do-it-yourself culture has ongoing appeal, and continues to attract makers and buyers.

By working with other local creatives, Andrea is able to tap into a variety of resources, including a collaboration with Think & Ink Studio to create custom fabric. With her understanding of being both a producer and a promoter, Andrea is an informed and active advocate of craft.

Crafting wherever she travels, Andrea Tong-Tucker picks up materials everywhere she goes, making keepsakes out of functional storage tins.

Simple Zip Pouch

ANDREA TONG-TUCKER

Many people are wary of sewing zips, but once the technique is conquered sewists can go on to explore other methods of application and fabric types. This fully lined, versatile pouch is perfect for carrying all kinds of items, and makes a great gift. The finished size is 20 x 16cm *(7⅛ x 6¼in)*.

1.

Position the Zip

Iron the fabric, then iron the shiny side of the interfacing to the wrong side of the fabric. Place one piece of the outer fabric with one piece of the lining fabric, right sides facing.

Sandwich the closed zip face down, with the opening pointing to left as shown, between the two layers of fabric and line up the top of the zip with the top of the fabric so that all pieces make a rectangle.

MATERIALS

Two pieces of outer fabric, 21 x 17cm *(8¼ x 6¾in)*.

Two pieces of iron-on interfacing, 21 x 17cm *(8¼ x 6¾in)*.

Two pieces of lining fabric, 21 x 17cm *(8¼ x 6¾in)*.

17.5cm *(7in)* zip.

Sewing machine and zipper foot.

General Knowledge

It is essential to use a standard zipper foot when sewing a zip with exposed teeth. As you approach the zip pull, leave the needle in the fabric, lift the zipper foot and remove it. Open the zip past the needle, then replace the foot, lower it and continue sewing.

A bamboo point turner is a great help with creating neat corners. Use it to push the corners out gently from the inside.

The right side of the fabric is the side that is printed. If you are using gingham, there is no right or wrong side.

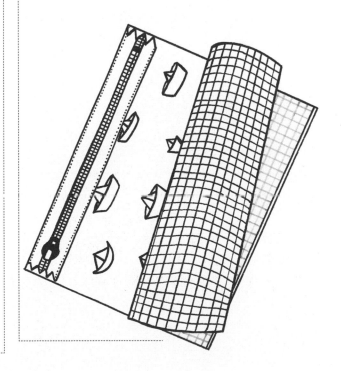

2.

Sew the Zip
Attach the zipper foot on your sewing machine and carefully sew all pieces together. Be aware of the zip pull.

3.

Complete the Zip
Repeat the process for the other side of the zip, making sure that the right sides of the outer fabric are together and the right sides of the inside fabric are together. Trim any loose threads.

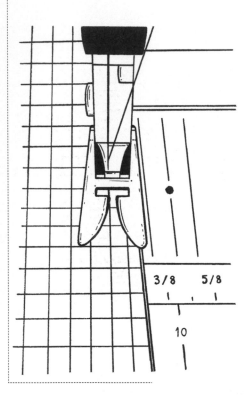

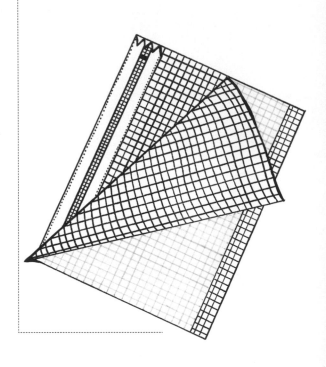

4.

Sew the Purse

Open the zip halfway. Fold the fabric so that the outer right sides face each other, and pin together. Do the same with the inner fabric.

Replace the zipper foot with the standard one and stitch around all four sides of the pouch with a 1cm *(⅜in)* seam allowance, leaving a 7.5cm *(3in)* opening at the bottom of the lining. When sewing the ends of the zip, be careful not to go through the teeth.

5.

Turn Right Side Out

Trim excess fabric and any loose ends. Turn the pouch to the right side by pushing the lining through the bottom. Push all four corners out and sew the opening closed either by machine or with small hand stitches.

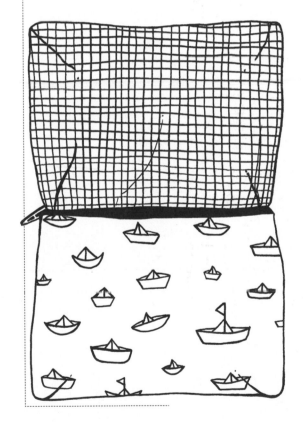

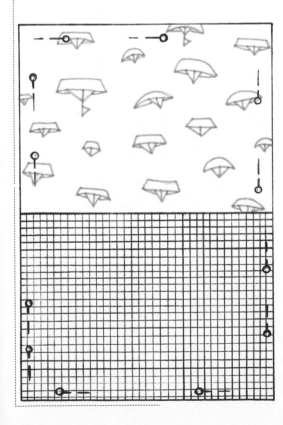

Sarai Mitnick

Colette Patterns

Sarai Mitnick is fascinated by vintage dressmaking, the fundamentals of how clothing is constructed and the detail that makes a garment feel special. Each pattern she invents is evocative of a style from the past, a product of keen research and an ability not only to recreate a garment but also to translate the process to a pattern that the modern dressmaker can work with.

Sarai understands the importance of accurate fit, and recognizes that even a pattern intended to suit modern sizing will need to be adapted. The patterns act as a teaching tool, providing home sewists with the opportunity to develop their understanding of how clothing is put together and how it can be made to flatter.

As a textile enthusiast, with an understanding of drape, weight and fibre, Sarai can make informed design decisions. Her dedication to experimenting with dressmaking techniques acts as a catalyst for the continued creation of new ideas, and in this way she is able to challenge every level of sewist, including herself.

Colette Patterns is based in Portland, Oregon. In a bright and airy studio, Sarai has created an environment conducive to creativity. She collaborates with local artists, designers, photographers and models to support the authentic feel of her products.

Sarai's patterns act as a springboard for home sewers to add their own design details and select fabrics that reflect their style and individuality. The impact of this approach is apparent in the community of amateur sewers who apply their own ideas to each pattern, sharing their results online. Sarai's work fosters curiosity among her audience to expand their stitching repertoire and create a personal handmade wardrobe.

Planning new patterns and selecting textiles; mood boards and sample garments hang in the Colette Patterns studio.

Sorbetto Top with Tucks

SARAI MITNICK

The Sorbetto is a versatile garment, with the additional fabric in the front pleat providing the perfect opportunity for all levels of sewist to add detail or practise manipulating fabric. Tucks are a simple way to add detail, with the option to add buttons and trimmings to suit your style. Choose soft white cotton for a romantic look, or for a tailored option work in silk dupioni. The Sorbetto also works beautifully in Liberty cotton lawn.

MATERIALS

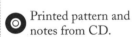 Printed pattern and notes from CD.

Lightweight fabric, 1.4m *(1½yd)*.

Sewing machine.

Sewing thread.

Two colours of marking pen, pencil or chalk.

Three small decorative buttons (optional).

1.25cm *(½in)* bias binding, 2.75m *(3yd)*.

1.

Cut Out Pattern Pieces and Mark

Cut out the pattern pieces, including the large pleat at the front. Do not mark the position of the pleat line, as that is the area where you will form the tucks.

Mark the centre front of the pattern, which is cut on the fold, with a vertical pin or fabric marker.

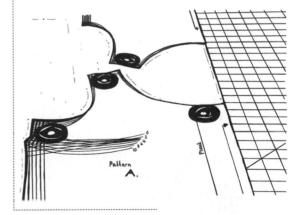

2.

Stay Stitch Neckline
Stay stitching the neckline will prevent the fabric from stretching; the stitches will not be seen. Sew a mid-length stitch around the neckline, approximately 3mm *(⅛in)* from the edge.

3.

Mark Out: Colour 1
Lay the front out flat. Using one colour, draw a line on each side of the centre front line, 1.25cm *(½in)* from the centre. You should now have two lines going up the front of your top on either side of the centre front.

   In the same colour, draw another line 2.5cm *(1in)* out from the first line. Repeat on the other side. Do this twice more, each time measuring 2.5cm *(1in)* away from the previous lines. You should have eight lines in the same colour, four on each side of the centre.

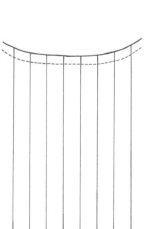

4.

Mark Out: Colour 2
Using the second colour, draw a line each side of the centre, this time 2.5cm *(1in)* out on either side. Repeat as you did with the first colour, measuring 2.5cm *(1in)* from the previous line each time, until you have four lines of the second colour on each side – eight in total.

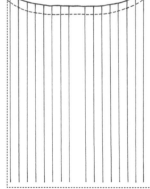

5.

Pin and Sew Tucks

With wrong sides together, bring the outermost line of the second colour to meet the next line in the first colour, and pin. This forms a tuck on the right side of the garment. Stitch the tuck in place down the marked line, about 6mm *(¼in)* from the fold of the tuck. Repeat for three more tucks on that side.

Do the same on the other side, making sure the tucks are pointing outwards.

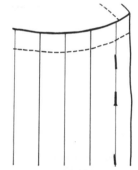

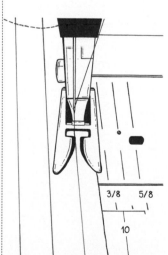

6.

Press

Press each tuck flat, then press away from the centre front.

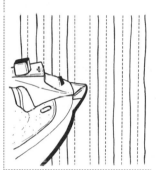

7.

Add Buttons and Finish

Attach three small buttons down the centre front, if liked. For an extra flourish, you could add covered buttons to match the main fabric or the bias binding.

Finish the top by following the instructions from the pattern.

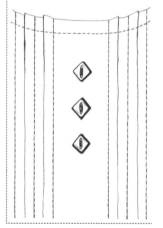

General Knowledge

When dressmaking, it is a good idea to make a toile, a simple version of a garment made in a low-cost fabric. This enables you to make changes to the fit without wasting a more precious material.

Once you have created a toile, refer to the Colette Patterns website (colettepatterns.com) for tutorials on sewing techniques, including working with tucks and how to make bust adjustments.

When printing the digital pattern, make sure you print the test square first to ensure that your pattern will print at the right size. Pay close attention when cutting out and again when taping together. It is worth spending the time getting the pattern right, as it can be used many times.

Address Book

The Sewists

Anna Alicia: aalicia.bigcartel.com

Kate Bowles: folksy.com/shops/KateBowles

Donna Bramhall, Spinster's Emporium/ HaberdasherMe: spinstersemporium.com

Abigail Brown: abigail-brown.co.uk

Sarah Burford, Curious Pip: curiouspip.com

Kim Davis, Oh, Sweet Joy: ohsweetjoy.com

Louise Evans, Felt Mistress: feltmistress.com

Rachelle Francis: rachellefrancis.com

Jessica Hayes-Gill: jessicahayesgill.com

Megan Hunt: princesslasertron.com

Julie Jackson, Subversive Cross Stitch®: subversivecrossstitch.com

Jaime Jennings and Amber Corcoran, Fancy Tiger Crafts: fancytigercrafts.com

Hannah Kopacz, Made with Love by Hannah: madewithlovebyhannah.com

Sarai Mitnick, Colette Patterns: colettepatterns.com

Josephine Perry: ourjosephine.co.uk

Leanne Sarah Smith, Bobbin & Bumble: folksy.com/shops/bobbinandbumble

Kirsty Southam, Me Plus Molly: meplusmolly.co.uk

Sophie Strong: sophiestrong.co.uk

Andrea Tong-Tucker, Roxypop: roxypop.ca

Katie Wagstaff, Oh Squirrel: ohsquirrel.co.uk

Fabric and Haberdashery Supplies

UK

Alfies Antique Market, London: alfiesantiques.com

Beyond Fabrics, London: beyond-fabrics.co.uk

Cloth House, London: clothhouse.com

Fringe, London: studio108.org

Joel & Son Fabrics, London: joelandsonfabrics.com

Paper and String, online shop: www.paper-and-string.co.uk

Ray-Stitch, London: raystitch.co.uk

Rolls & Rems, London: rollsandrems.com

Leon's Fabric Superstore, Manchester: leonsfabrics.co.uk

Anglian Fashion Fabrics, Norwich: anglianfashionfabrics.co.uk

Crafts and Quilts, Southport: craftsandquilts.net

International

Spool of Thread, Vancouver, Canada: spoolofthread.com

The Workroom, Toronto, Canada: theworkroom.ca

Johanna Daimer, Munich, Germany: daimer-filze.com

Tokyu Hands, Japan: tokyu-hands.co.jp

Mood Designer Fabrics, New York and Los Angeles, USA: moodfabrics.com

Bolt, Portland, USA: boltfabricboutique.com

Fabric Depot, Portland, USA: fabricdepot.com

Hawthorne Threads: hawthornethreads.com

Eco Supplies

Offset Warehouse: offsetwarehouse.com

Organic Cotton: organiccotton.biz

Bookbinding Supplies

Shepherds, London: falkiners.com

Ratchford, Stockport: ratchford.co.uk

Eco-Craft: eco-craft.co.uk

Printing Supplies

UK
Cass Art, London: cassart.co.uk

International
Dharma Trading Co: dharmatrading.com

The sewists also recommend scouring markets, charity and thrift shops, car-boot sales, Etsy (etsy.com), Folksy (folksy.com) and online auction sites for equipment and materials.

For Seb

Acknowledgements

Firstly, a huge thank you to the designer-makers who generously took part in the project, welcoming me into their studios, homes and creative worlds, and fuelling my enthusiasm with their original ideas.

Thanks to Judith Isherwood and the team at Fringe for providing a fantastic photo-shoot location, and to Sam Walton for his photography skills. Thank you to Helen Rochester and Clare Double for making this book a reality, and to illustrator Lily Tennant and designer Jane Chipchase-Bates for realizing the pages.

Finally, but not lastly, thank you Mum: for making sewing at home part of the everyday and always being proud of my creations.